The Search for Meaning
in Organizations

The Search for Meaning in Organizations

Seven Practical Questions for Ethical Managers

MOSES L. PAVA

QUORUM BOOKS
Westport, Connecticut • London

Library of Congress Cataloging-in-Publication Data

Pava, Moses L.
   The search for meaning in organizations : seven practical
questions for ethical managers / Moses L. Pava.
     p. cm.
   Includes bibliographical references and index.
   ISBN 1–56720–201–2 (alk. paper)
   1. Business ethics. 2. Corporations—Moral and ethical aspects.
3. Corporations—Religious aspects. 4. Social responsibility of
business. I. Title.
HF5387.P385   1999
174'.4—dc21   99–10407

British Library Cataloguing in Publication Data is available.

Library of Congress Catalog Card Number: 99–10407
ISBN: 1–56720–201–2

First published in 1999

Quorum Books, 88 Post Road West, Westport, CT 06881
An imprint of Greenwood Publishing Group, Inc.
www.quorumbooks.com

Printed in the United States of America

The paper used in this book complies with the
Permanent Paper Standard issued by the National
Information Standards Organization (Z39.48–1984).

10 9 8 7 6 5 4 3 2 1

Copyright Acknowledgments

The author and publisher are grateful for permission to reproduce portions of the following copyrighted material:

Badaracco, Joseph L., Jr. 1997. *Defining Moments: When Managers Must Choose Between Right and Right*. Boston: Harvard Business School Press. Reprinted with permission.

McCoy, Bowen. September/October 1983. "The Parable of the Sadhu." *Harvard Business Review*, Vol. 61. Reprinted in Peter Madsen and Jay M. Shafritz, eds., *Essentials of Business Ethics*. New York: Penguin Books, 1990, pp. 190–200. Reprinted with permission.

Walton, Clarence. 1967. *Corporate Social Responsibilities*. Belmont, CA: Wadsworth. Copyright © 1967. Reprinted with permission.

To my children,
Rebecca, Jonah, and Micah

Contents

Acknowledgments

Although this book is a deeply personal statement, it is also a product of the numerous communities of which I am a member. Without the help and encouragement of my colleagues, friends, and family members, this work would not have been possible.

First, I would like to thank the administration, faculty, and students at Yeshiva University, a truly great, meaning-based organization. I am grateful to Dr. Harold Nierenberg, Dean of the Sy Syms School of Business, for creating and sustaining an environment conducive to seeing this project through to its conclusion. His understanding and assistance have gone beyond the call of duty. In addition, I thank the President of Yeshiva University, Dr. Norman Lamm, and the Vice President of Academic Affairs (recently retired), Dr. William Schwartz, for their continued support and unstinting encouragement. I thank my colleagues here at the Syms School, especially Drs. Joel Hochman, Joshua Krausz, and Marty Lebowitz. One way or another, each of these three people has contributed greatly to the finished product. I have also benefited much from the many students I have had the pleasure of teaching. I would like to formally thank two: Joseph Weilgus and Yosef Levine. Both of them volunteered numerous hours in helping me to prepare this manuscript.

In addition, I would like to thank Patrick Primeaux and Jeremy Pava. Both of them have spent numerous hours discussing many of the issues raised here. I know they don't agree with all of my conclusions, but their input and feedback are greatly appreciated.

This book grew out of a paper I delivered in honor of Dr. Clarence Walton at American College during the spring of 1997. Both the original paper and this book are attempts to capture and extend his vision of business ethics, what he called the "artistic model." I am truly thankful for all of the help Dr. Walton has generously bestowed upon me over the last number of years.

Most importantly, I thank my helpmate, my soulmate, my best friend, my strongest critic, and my wife, Vivian Newman. My relationship with Vivian informs, strengthens, and gives meaning to everything that I do.

Finally, this book is dedicated to my children: Rebecca, Jonah, and Micah. Their curiosity, intelligence, love, sincerity, and passion for life light up our lives (and keep us busy) as we never could have imagined.

The Search for Meaning in Organizations

1

Introduction

If business ethics conjures up an image of an ever-growing and more inventive list of "thou shalts" and "thou shalt nots," it is because the business ethics movement has often been misunderstood. Business ethics is not about constraints; it is about purpose and human potential. The core idea upon which this book is built is that the power and success of business are ultimately dependent on managers' beliefs about life's meanings. It is no exaggeration to suggest that corporate success is set in motion and encouraged by a set of core ethical values shared by managers, employees, and other stakeholders.

While some general values are shared across corporations and cultures, others are unique to particular industries, organizations, and individuals. Until recently, core values were perceived as firm, lasting, and stable; describing them as being inscribed in stone really wasn't all that far off the mark. Handed down from generation to generation, core values were easily learned or at least acceptably mimicked with a minimum of thought. On the brink of the twenty-first century, this is hardly the case.

In fact, today it is recognized that there is no magic formula, other than hard work, to discover or invent these evolving core values. The only way to learn and use them is to talk about them with each other.

To talk about them sensibly, we must begin to organize our thoughts carefully. It is increasingly true that business managers view themselves as practical philosophers, poets, and storytellers, as much as they think of themselves as number crunchers. The best managers can distinguish between these distinct activities and jump effortlessly from one to the other.

The purpose of this book is straightforward: to help managers and everyone else who recognizes the central role of business to our culture to think systematically about business ethics. The book is organized around a set of seven practical, but open-ended, questions designed to stimulate thought about the importance of business to our lives and society. Each of the seven questions was selected with three specific purposes in mind. First, the question must probe a core area of business ethics; second, the question must help to reveal a unique aspect of the meaning-based organization; and third, each question must fit with the others to portray something greater than merely the sum of its parts. As the book unfolds, and we begin to offer answers to each of the seven questions, the concept of the meaning-based organization becomes three-dimensional and real.

These are the kinds of questions about which I often find myself reassuring students, "There's no one right answer." Nevertheless, we do distinguish between better and worse answers. This is not a recipe book where one looks to find the needed ingredients and the prescribed steps to be taken. It simply provides a way to initiate a helpful and meaningful conversation, with oneself and with others, about the significance of business and business ethics.

The ideas presented here are based on the rich and nuanced research in business ethics, including some of my own original work. But, more importantly, the book grows out of my continuous conversations with international business leaders, ethics officers, business ethics scholars, and business and theology students at Yeshiva University. If this text serves to help managers help themselves and others to integrate personal and organizational meaning with financial success, it will have achieved its goal.

2

What Is Business Ethics, Anyway?

In short, the country stands poised on the edge of developing a style of life that probes more deeply than the material and physical realm. Somehow, say the advocates of the artistic model (of corporate social responsibility), men are suddenly remembering what a typical renaissance man said to his fellow beings. Pico della Mirandola heard God saying to man:

"You alone are not bound by any restraint, unless you will adopt it by the will we have given you. I have placed you in the center of the world that you may the easier look about and behold all that is in it. I created you a creature, neither earthly nor heavenly, so that you could be your own creator and select whatever form you may choose for yourself." (Walton, 1967, p. 141)

When the subject turns to business ethics, it is not always clear what we're really talking about. Surely, nobody wants to wake up and read about herself or himself on the front page of the morning newspapers defending the indefensible. To the cynics, business ethics simply implies, "Don't get caught!" The corollary to this rule is if you do get caught, "Make sure you have an alibi."

Perhaps, the real business ethics discussion begins when we finally realize that even if we knew somehow that we would never get caught, and even if we could be assured that our humbled photos would never adorn the front pages of the newspapers, we would still *want* to talk about business ethics. But what is it that we would discuss? Or, as the title of this chapter asks, What is business ethics, anyway?

As with this question and the six to follow, there are no right and wrong answers. A one-size-fits-all approach advocated from on high simply can't work in today's modern, pluralistic organizations. Rather, the purpose of this book is to initiate a conversation, to begin a process. Discovering business ethics is not a job for tired government regulators, overactive business consultants, ponderous academics, or idealistic spiritual and religious leaders to do alone. In the final analysis, businessmen and businesswomen have to discover and rediscover for themselves the nature of business and business ethics. On the brink of the twenty-first century, understanding business ethics is fast becoming a primary task for business leaders and would-be leaders.

This introductory chapter helps to ground our thinking. No doubt the tentative suggestions offered here will be refined and polished as we take up some of the issues discussed in the later chapters, but we must begin somewhere. The most important point of this chapter is simply this: our understanding of business ethics is linked directly to our definition of business. We can't talk about business ethics unless we talk first about business. This chapter provides two very different definitions of business and shows how each definition provides the seeds for its own version of what business ethics is. One of the most important tasks for business managers is to think about how best to integrate these distinct views.

Most business managers are familiar with the first kind of business ethics, but not with the second. The first business ethics is much talked about in the popular media, business school courses, business ethics seminars, and the academic literature. The second business ethics, while hardly new, is much more elusive; while most people recognize it, they are hard-pressed to define it. In the first view, business is about *power*, and business ethics is about how best to constrain this power. Let's call the first kind of business ethics the *commodity-based* view. In the second view, business is about *meaning*, and business ethics is about how to pursue and interpret this meaning. We'll call this the *meaning-based* view.

Both business ethics are necessary. The first kind of business ethics without the second is like computer hardware without the software, a glistening, noble machine but with absolutely nothing significant to do.

The second view without the first is like software without the hardware, a brilliant and elegant idea but with nobody to think it.

THE COMMODITY-BASED VIEW

This more familiar view of the corporation suggests that business institutions are primarily devoted to producing and allocating goods and services to various stakeholder groups in society. Corporations or, more precisely, the members of corporations are exclusively concerned about the material well-being of society. This is not to say that in other aspects of their lives corporate players ignore nonmaterial concerns, but as participants in the corporation, these concerns are purposely and systematically ignored. The key to this view is that *before* individuals enter the corporate world, they know who they are and what they want. Preferences and identities are predetermined and, for the most part, unchanging. *According to the commodity-based view, the corporation is defined as an instrumental tool to satisfy established wants and preferences.*

Based on this definition, the primary business ethics question is how to share "fairly" the material goods and services (i.e., commodities) produced by the corporation—in light of given individual preferences and identities. In this view, business ethics is like the umpire at a tug-of-war contest. The umpire's job is to ensure that no one team gets an unfair advantage over any of the others. It is surely not the job of umpires to make up the rules of the contest as they go.

THE MEANING-BASED VIEW OF THE CORPORATION

The second definition of the corporation introduces the concept of ambiguity. The key to the second view is that while individuals tentatively enter the corporate world with answers to the questions about who they are and what they want, they also are well aware that the very act of participating in the business enterprise will itself undoubtedly affect these answers. Here, it is understood that while a corporation can satisfy established wants and preferences, as in the first view, the most important characteristic of the corporation resides in its ability to help create, nourish, and alter wants, preferences, and identities.

A definition of the corporation consistent with this view recognizes that the *corporation produces and allocates goods and services but insists that the primary characteristic is that it serves as a location where human beings interpret life's meanings.* In this alternative definition of the corporation, the human quest for meaning and significance takes center stage; corporate activity is understood as both instrumental and expressive.

A meaning-based view of the corporation points out that corporate players are ultimately more interested in symbols, ceremonies, stories, myths, and language than contracts, budgets, and annual reports. The key business ethics question, from this perspective, is not how to allocate commodities fairly but focuses attention on how meaning is interpreted and how symbols are understood and apportioned. As Stanford University professor James March (1994) has noted, "The reason people involved in decision making devote so much time to symbols, myths, and rituals is that they *care more about them*" (p. 218; emphasis added).

Where the commodity-based view of the corporation does not necessarily reject the notion of meaning outright, it seems to suggest minimally that it has no legitimate role to play within the firm boundaries of the corporation. The crucial point for the purposes of this chapter is that the meaning-based view, by contrast, suggests that any attempt to understand business ethics will, at best, be only partially successful if it ignores our expressive natures and our primary attachment to symbols. While corporate players are no doubt interested in increasing consumption, a myopic focus on consumption to the neglect of everything else yields a sparse conception of the corporation and its social responsibilities. In this view, business ethics takes center stage and is best thought of not as an umpire at a tug-of-war contest but as the author of a dramatic play. Here, the responsibilities are great, but so is the ultimate payoff.

BUSINESS IS BUSINESS: BUSINESS ETHICS AND THE COMMODITY-BASED VIEW

Most of us, most of the time, look at business through the commodity-based lens. Business is action-oriented. Defining the corporation in this way does not necessarily entail an amoral view of the business corporation. The best example of a business ethics built upon a commodity-based view of the corporation is the now-familiar "stakeholder theory." Numerous books and articles have adopted a stakeholder framework.

These writers suggest that corporations must recognize responsibilities to various stakeholder groups in society, beyond stockholders. The word "stakeholder" is used as a conscious play on the word "stockholder." These obligations minimally consist of responsibilities (1) to customers to produce safe, high-quality products at reasonable prices, (2) to suppliers to treat them honestly and with integrity, (3) to employees and managers to provide profitable work opportunities and to be rewarded in an open and just way, (4) to local, national, and global communities to be good corporate citizens, and (5) to shareholders and creditors to earn a fair return on invested capital. Although the model has been interpreted and advocated as a purely descriptive theory of the corporation or as an instrumental view, it undoubtedly also has normative aspirations. The clearest and least equivocal statement of this characteristic of the theory has been given recently by Thomas Donaldson and Lee Preston (1995).

Although it is difficult, if not impossible, to produce a once-and-for-all list of the critical issues related to business ethics, the stakeholder theory provides a useful framework for investigating and pinpointing corporate responsibilities while at the same time providing a convenient "club" to wield to remind us that stockholders are not the only legitimate stakeholders. Further, the theory allows us to examine such responsibilities without abandoning the commodity-based view. That this is the case is obvious in the Donaldson–Preston formulation, where they simply take it as self-evident that stakeholders come to the table with known "interests," and, in fact, the authors explicitly claim that stakeholders are identified by these preexisting "interests" in the corporation. The stakeholder theory denies outright the possibility for ambiguity in decision making, which is, of course, at the heart of the meaning-based view. As the stakeholder theory has developed thus far, the picture of the corporation that emerges is better thought of as "a tool designed to satisfy established wants and preferences" than "as a location where human beings interpret life's meanings."

Accordingly, stakeholder theorists must necessarily conduct the business ethics debate under cover of the large shadow of existing power relationships. In fact, stakeholder theory and the commodity-based view of the corporation upon which it is built would seem to suggest that the substance of business is about gaining and using power to promote one's own interests. The commodity-based view, with its static view of human preferences and identities and its rejection of the notion of ambiguity, would not seem to leave much room for anything else. Here, learning, human development, community, and individual and organizational transformations are meaningless constructs. Power, defined classically as "the possibility of imposing one's will upon the behavior of other persons" (Weber, 1954, p. 232), is the ultimate currency in which business transactions are conducted. Care should be taken here to emphasize that this is not to suggest that power relationships are not to be constrained by perceived corporate social responsibilities. From a stakeholder view, Donaldson and Preston are surely correct when they insist that "each group of stakeholders merits consideration for its own sake" and that stakeholders are "persons or groups with legitimate interests in . . . aspects of corporate activity." But, in essence, corporate social responsibilities, properly conceived, are *constraints* on the fundamental "corporate activity" of business—which is to exercise power. When one finally opens up the black box into which most stakeholder theorists locate business, what one finds is naked power. *Stakeholder theory views this power as legitimate if and only if it is appropriately constrained.*

Defining corporate social responsibilities as "power constraints" is meant to encompass a wide range of alternative suggestions with regard to the proper contours of corporate social responsibilities. Consider Clarence Walton's classic typology of corporate social responsibilities as outlined in his widely respected 1967 book:

A—*The Austere Model*—The only legitimate group of stakeholders are stockholders. The only social responsibility of management is to vigorously and unapologetically pursue stockholders' interests.

B—*The Household Model*—Human resources are a firm's most precious asset. Anything that depersonalizes employees or assigns them a low rating in the corporation's list of priorities is to be rejected as unsound. In this view, the claims of both managers and blue-collar workers are potentially superior to those of stockholders.

C—*The Vendor Model*—Consumers are the forgotten people of modern economics. "Forgotten because big business and big unions have produced a species of accommodations where the rewards of increased productivity are shared with these groups rather than with the consumer" (Walton, 1967, p. 132). This model suggests the illegitimacy of "deliberately engineered product obsolescence, shoddy service on consumer durables, excessive and hidden charges for credit, and the withholding of new products from the market" (Walton, 1967, p. 133).

D—*The Investment Model*—Stretching the notion of stakeholders beyond shareholders, employees, and customers, this view defends corporate charitable donations to universities and other groups useful to the corporation. Such giving is defended strictly in terms of the firm's enlightened self-interest.

E—*The Civic Model*—Shareholders are not the owners of the corporation. "In a sense, possessors of liquid property do not own the corporation, for they can pull out at a moment's notice, they do not nourish or care for any real property, and they seek only their own gain without concern for the social responsibilities attached to all real property. Hence, the corporation has a responsibility to the industrial system and the political system, which is the former's protective mantle" (Walton, 1967, p. 137). Among other implications, this view suggests corporations should attempt to alleviate unemployment and dampen chronic business cycles. (A sixth model, the artistic model, is discussed later.)

The scope and reach of these five models are great. In each case, Walton emphasizes an alternative stakeholder group with a legitimate claim on the corporation. After carefully identifying these claims, proper *constraints* are called for. In some cases, governmental solutions are demanded, and in other cases discretion is given to managerial decision makers. For example, in the household model, Walton notes, "Legally, a corporation must recognize the rights of employees to organize and bargain collectively, must bargain in good faith, and must honor the collective agreements produced through such bargaining. The model rejects, however, the view "that the ethical obligation of corporate employers of consequence . . . is equated with their legal obligation" (Walton, 1967, p. 130). Walton emphasizes, in this case, that the law is an incomplete guide to social responsibilities.

As different as these "stakeholder" models are, unquestionably, the common thread that runs through all five of them is the underlying definition of the corporation as a utilitarian tool designed to satisfy established wants and preferences among the various stakeholder groups. The models present and emphasize alternative formulations for legitimately constraining corporate power, but the fundamental assumption that stakeholders are solely interested in power, as in all commodity-based views, is never seriously brought into question. Even in the household and civic models (which border on a meaning-based conception), the relevant stakeholders are still primarily seen to be struggling against one another to promote their own preconceived interests. In the household model, the corporation needs to be structured in such a way as to ensure that employees get what's coming to them. "The assertion of the claims may be vigorous in some industries and through some unions and relatively weak in others" (Walton, 1967, p. 131). But it is taken as self-evident that the key activity is "the assertion of claims." Similarly, even the civic model is primarily defended more in terms of constraining power than in building a republican democracy. Walton cites Adolf Berle's view as representative of the civic model:

You make money, yes. But you don't know what your efforts cost the community around you. If those costs were added to your cost, businesses very much in the black now would find themselves in the red—and vice-versa. This means, in substance, that we are all cogs in a vast machine. Sometimes the cogs are very big—but big or little there is no escape from your being in the machine. (as quoted in Walton, 1967, p. 138)

Walton himself emphasizes the precise distinction we are making here by noting, in regard to the civic model, "Public-mindedness does not necessarily produce public-spiritedness, and social consciousness is not social conscience" (p. xx). In Walton's view, "public-mindedness" and "social consciousness" can be understood as commodity-based concepts, whereas "public-spiritedness" and "social-conscience" require a meaning-based view.

The commodity-based view of the corporation holds a powerful sway on our thinking. It emphasizes the distinctiveness of the economic sphere and suggests that we can set hard-and-fast boundaries around the business enterprise. The cliché "business is business" is apt here.

Don't underestimate the commodity-based view. It represents a fantastic invention that has unleashed the great potential for economic growth and human development that had lain dormant for centuries. No longer do religious authorities unilaterally set the just price and enforce fair profits. Michael Novak (1982) describes the huge benefits of drawing well-marked boundaries as follows:

It is a distinctive invention of democratic capitalism to have conceived a way of differentiating three major spheres of life, and to have assigned to each relatively autonomous networks of institutions. This differentiation of systems sets individuals possessed of the will-to-power on three separate tracks. Political activists may compete for eminence in the political system, economic activists in the economic system, religious activists and intellectuals in various parts of the moral-cultural system. But the powers of each of the three systems over the others, while in each case substantial, are firmly limited. (p. 56)

No doubt, many of today's and tomorrow's business ethics issues will and should be framed and ultimately decided in language drawn strictly from the commodity-based view. Consider the following questions consistent with the five models.

A—*The Austere Model*—How much information are shareholders entitled to?

Item 1: Shoney's, the big restaurant chain which settled one of the nation's largest racial discrimination lawsuits in 1992, is at the center of a debate between large investors and the Securities and Exchange Commission over shareholder resolutions about workplace issues. Shareholders have called for a vote on a proposal at Shoney's Inc.'s annual meeting. The measure, if approved, would require Shoney's to account publicly for its efforts since 1994 to reverse discriminatory purchase practices (*New York Times*, December 26, 1996).

B—*The Household Model*—Who are the members of the "household," and who decides?

Item 2: One of the nation's largest supermarket chains agreed yesterday to pay $81.5 million to settle accusations that it systematically denied promotions, raises and preferred assignments to *women*. . . . The company admitted to no wrong doing . . . saying it was in full compliance with all fair-employment laws (*New York Times*, January 25, 1997; emphasis added).

Item 3: Federal law suits in which large numbers of employees team up to complain of systematic racial, sexual, and age discrimination by their companies have more than doubled in the last four years. The suits now cover at least 100,000 employees, according to authorities on employee discrimination (*New York Times*, January 12, 1997).

Item 4: As hospitals merge and shrink under pressure from managed care, a large and growing number of senior doctors and nurses have found themselves suddenly dismissed or demoted at the height of their careers. With their high salaries and roots in old-style medicine, older doctors and nurses are natural targets for hospitals trying desperately to economize, health experts say (*New York Times*, January 26, 1997).

C—*The Vendor Model*—Are some products so dangerous that they should be taken off the market completely? If these products remain on the market, to what extent do managers of these corporations have to disclose the known dangers to customers and other interested parties?

Item 5: It was very difficult when you were asked, as chairman of a tobacco company, to discuss the health question on television. You had not only your own business to consider but the employees throughout the industry, retailers, consumers, farmers growing the leaf, and so on, and you were in much too responsible a position to get up and say: "I accept that the product which we and all our competitors are putting on the market gives you lung cancer; whatever you might think privately" (Anthony D. McCormick, former chairman of Batco, as quoted by the *New York Times*, June 16, 1994).

D—*The Investment Model*—Is "strategic philanthropy" still philanthropy?

Item 6: Philanthropic and business units have joined forces to develop giving strategies that increase their name recognition among consumers, boost employee productivity, reduce R&D costs, overcome regulatory obstacles, and foster synergy among business units. In short, the strategic use of philanthropy has begun to give companies a powerful competitive edge (Smith, 1994, p. 105).

E—*The Civic Model*—To what extent can society rely upon business corporations to "factor in" environmental impacts? To what degree should corporations be allowed to participate in political campaigns?

Item 7: Corporations are recognizing the benefits to the community *and to their long term corporate profitability* of reducing environmental impacts. Environmental protection and economic growth have become closely aligned, both in the growth of the environmental technologies business and the movement to reduce environmental impacts, improve production efficiency, and reduce costs (Epstein, 1996; see p. xxv).

Item 8: Corporations vigorously participate in the political process, donating huge sums of money to candidates and parties and taking out op-ed type advertisements in major U.S. newspapers. Not only are corporations expected to play by the rules, but corporations help make the rules.

The preceding questions and items, culled from the popular media, are meant to be illustrative (rather than exhaustive) of the kinds of issues that currently dominate (and will no doubt continue to dominate for the foreseeable future) the business ethics agenda. All of the items listed comfortably fit with the commodity-based view of the corporation. The business ethics question that is repeated each time is how to allocate fairly the corporation's output (including goods, services, employment opportunities, etc.) among competing stakeholders. Each of these issues potentially calls for a particular kind of constraint on existing power relationships. Should the Securities and Exchange Commission (SEC) and investors constrain managers to produce more and better disclosures? What is the best and most efficient way for women, minorities, and the elderly to gain and hold a fair share of the corporate pie? To what extent should customers' rights be protected? Can corporations help meet communities' needs while they simultaneously justify corporate giving in terms of overcoming "regulatory obstacles"? Will market-based arguments constrain managers to protect the environment? These questions all assume that business is about power and that business ethics is about how best to constrain this power.

THE PURSUIT OF SOMETHING MORE: BUSINESS ETHICS AND THE MEANING-BASED VIEW

Consider the following simple scenario:

A young child visits his friend, bringing with him a brand-new, brightly colored ball. After a short time his friend becomes jealous watching him joyously throw the ball high into the air and catching it. The friend exclaims, "It's my house.

While you're here, you have to let me play with the ball." The first child responds, "It's my ball and I want to play with it by myself!" The mother of the friend, watching from the kitchen window, ponders her decision. "I do have another ball I could give them to play with or perhaps I could teach them to play a game of catch with the one ball."

Most people of whom I have asked this question (from the very young to the very old) recognize the first solution as a practical possibility but believe that the second solution is somehow "ethically" superior. What is it about the second solution that elicits an almost universal recognition of its superiority?

I think examples like this one illustrate our need to find a "language of ought" beyond purely formal and legalistic pronouncements. "Ethics talk" may be soft and fuzzy, as its critics happily note, but the vocabulary of ethics intimates a "meaning" dimension beyond the material level. Vaclav Havel, president of the Czech and Slovak Federal Republic, is one of the world's few politicians to have recognized this need for expanding our political vocabulary:

I am convinced that we will never build a democratic state based on rule of law if we do not at the same time build a state that is—regardless of how unscientific this may sound to the ears of a political scientist—humane, moral, intellectual and spiritual, and cultural. The best laws and the best-conceived democratic mechanisms will not in themselves guarantee legality or freedom or human right—anything, in short for which they were intended—if they are not underpinned by certain human and social values. (Havel, 1992, p. 218)

While Havel is talking about the state, our interest is primarily at the level of the business organization. The meaning-based view of the corporation agrees with the commodity-based view that business is about power. But, contrary to the commodity-based view, it would suggest that it is not only about power. James March (1994) provides the most articulate description of decision making as understood from a meaning-based perspective. His view is worth quoting:

As the construction of meaning has been explored . . . , the argument has been developed that a choice process does many things beyond providing a basis for action. It provides an occasion for defining virtue and truth, for discovering or interpreting what is happening, what decision makers have been doing, and what justifies their actions. (p. 218)

At first glance a meaning-based view of the corporation consistent with March's description might seem quite esoteric and so at odds with the way we normally think about business and business decision making that its importance might, at best, be described as marginal and of little significance in the real world. A little reflection, though, about the nature of advertising contradicts this conclusion. In fact, most marketing experts, with the responsibility for expending billions of dollars per year on advertising, would seem to accept something like the meaning-based view discussed here. Is Coca-Cola selling more than a high-fructose, carbonated beverage? When people buy automobiles, are they merely purchasing transportation? These questions, of course, answer themselves. Marketing experts know that business is not only about dividing up the pie but about providing an opportunity to explore, discover, and display meaning. That the "meaning" inherent in these two examples may not offer the best in human thinking (to say the least) in no way undercuts the important observation that the commodity-based view with its insistence that preferences are stable has significant limitations in explaining much business behavior. If marketing experts can adopt (and exploit) something like the meaning-based view of the corporation, surely business ethics-minded managers should examine its implications.

An essential point of the meaning-based view of the corporation is its insistence that preferences and identities are shaped and influenced by humanely constructed business institutions. There is a dialectic at work here that suggests that, on one hand, human beings create business institutions, but, on the other hand, business institutions help create human beings. The commodity-based view recognizes only the first part of this formulation. Perhaps the most famous statement of this dialectic, in a more general context, is by Peter Berger and Thomas Luckmann in their often-cited work *The Social Construction of Reality*:

Identity is formed by social processes. Once crystallized, it is maintained, modified, or even reshaped by social relations. The social processes involved in both the formation and the maintenance of identity are determined by the social structure. Conversely, the identities produced by the interplay of organism, individual consciousness and social structure react upon the given social structure, maintaining it, modifying it, or even reshaping it. Societies have histories in the course of which specific identities emerge; these histories are, however, made by men with specific identities. (1967, p. 173)

A major goal of this chapter is to explore some of the implications of these ideas for understanding the future of business ethics.

The notion of a meaning-based perspective is not new. It is, for example, consistent with Clarence Walton's sixth model of corporate social responsibility:

F—*The Artistic Model*—"Indistinct, rudimentary, but perceptibly present in the statements of corporate executives and, to a lesser degree, in their actions is a kind of social responsibility that can be explained only in terms of a new approach, which is called the "artistic model" (p. 139).

Walton notes that the spirit of the artistic model is best captured by Neil Chamberlain in the following quote:

The real managerial satisfaction must come in conjuring up ways in which this organization . . . can now be used by you to accomplish objectives beyond the imagination and *even beyond the interests of those who form its several parts.* . . . The managers to whom we tend to give the accolades are—as in the case of the artist—those who can accomplish their functions while building into their work some purely personal expression, which will be the mark of their uniqueness and vision. (as quoted in Walton, 1967, pp. 38–48; emphasis added)

Walton, following Chamberlain, suggests that, at least according to one view of the corporation, the goal is not to accumulate and exercise maximum power but to create a medium to explore and communicate a meaningful human expression.

A major implication of this chapter is that a meaning-based view of the corporation alters significantly our understanding of business ethics. To some extent the impacts and controversies of the meaning-based view have already begun to emerge. Consider the following items:

Item 9: Close to 4,000 companies (including RJR Nabisco Holdings, Hudson Foods Inc., and Hall Graphics) are overcoming their misgivings and are hiring ordained Christian ministers and priests to tend to their employees' emotional and spiritual needs, even as they will publicly admit (as Hudson Foods Inc. explicitly does) that such practices represent a "financial drain" on the company. The Dallas Theological Seminary now offers the first master's degree program for corporate chaplains. "Although nearly all the active industrial chaplains are Christian, most companies insist they leave their religious affiliations and any penchant for preaching at the plant door" (*New York Times*, October 3, 1996).

Item 10: In response to the more than 250 million children under age 14 who are currently working in developing countries (according to a United Nations estimate), the notion of "fair trade" seems to be taking hold. According to Mimi Stephens, the executive director of the Fair Trade Federation, the group now includes 95 American organizations. These organizations work in different ways. Some will buy crafts and clothing only from factories in developing countries which follow acceptable labor practices. Any profits are returned to the producers. Other organizations simply certify that the commodity was produced under fair and reasonable conditions. Still others, like big sporting goods manufacturers, will set and enforce minimum standards like banning child labor or convict labor (*New York Times*, December 25, 1996).

Item 11: The NFL [National Football League] wants to use its valuable post–Super Bowl prime-time television spot for presentation ceremonies and player interviews focused on the game. In spite of the controversy, Reggie White of the Green Bay Packers uses his time to offer a prayer to God.

Item 12: The *New York Times* asserts that progress in the day care industry will be at best piecemeal. After recognizing the high cost of day care, the article concludes that "the largest impediment of change is Americans' failure to acknowledge, for better and worse, that the 1950's world of 'Leave It to Beaver,' and 'Father Knows Best,' is history and that Mom is working outside the home for good. Until attitudes reflect the reality, day care is likely to remain the latchkey kid of public policy" (*New York Times*, December 25, 1996).

No matter what side one takes in these controversies—whether or not one advocates corporate ministers, "fair trade," prime-time prayers, or industrial day care—it should be obvious that these issues are different in kind from those items cited in the previous section.

The preceding examples demonstrate that while the business corporation produces and allocates goods and services, it also serves as a location where human beings interpret life. People care deeply about these issues not because such care necessarily promotes preconceived interests but because the resolution of these issues will ultimately impact who we are and who we are becoming. Peter Drucker noted recently, "Not so long ago, we talked about 'labor'; increasingly, now we are talking of 'human resources'" (1993, p. 66). Will corporations (Item 9) and sports leagues (Item 11) evolve further and formally and bureaucratically recognize that employees are not just "human resources" but also human beings with religious and spiritual aspirations and needs? Consumers, manufacturers, regulators, and others care about fair trade (Item 10) not only as a means of constraining the power of big business but because the resolution of this issue will symbolize and teach us much about the meaning of business. Any attempt to resolve the disputes about day care must surely recognize that this debate is not only about "who gets what," but, in the final analysis, it is about how we and our children will choose to interpret the meanings of our lives.

Unquestionably, the meaning-based view of the corporation complicates the corporate social responsibility debate by significantly enlarging our understanding of what a corporation is. Here, the corporation finally bursts out of the familiar boundaries of the commodity-based view. Because it complicates the business ethics debate, some have argued that it is not a practical approach for business managers. If one of the goals of business ethics is to help managers resolve "real-world" ethical dilemmas (as it surely is), it is fatal to the business ethics enterprise to prove that it is not "pragmatic." Andrew Stark (1993), for example, has criticized business ethicist Norman Bowie's powerful suggestion that the primary obligation of the business enterprise is "to provide *meaningful* work for . . . employees" on precisely these grounds (Bowie, 1991, p. 18; emphasis added). Stark writes, "Even if one believes this assertion to be true, such a claim is so alien to the institutional world inhabited by most managers that it becomes impossible for them to act on it" (1993, p. 46). Stark's criticism, however, is deeply flawed. If the corporation was only an instrumental tool to satisfy wants and preferences, as the commodity-based view suggests, perhaps he would be correct. What Stark fails to recognize explicitly, however, is that corporations are also locations where meaning is actively interpreted. Business ethicists haven't "taken in the world of practice" (Stark, 1993, p. 43) because they recognize that interpretations on the meaning of business are continually being contested by sophisticated stakeholders, rather than taken as self-evident. From this perspective, of course, Bowie's suggestion becomes a plausible and practical understanding for the purpose of the business corporation. For Stark's criticisms to hold, what he really must state and defend (but never does) is that the commodity-based view better describes the corporation than the meaning-based view. By ignoring the notion of something like the meaning-based corporation and implicitly advocating the commodity-based view, Stark's conclusions come perilously close to being a mere tautology. If business ethics were only about power constraints, Bowie's suggestion would, of course, make little sense. If, however, managers and other stakeholders are aware of the symbolic and expressive characteristics of decision making, Bowie's counsel becomes a logical and acceptable extension. Stark wants to put the "meaning" genie back into the bottle; at minimum, he needs to carefully explain how he plans to do it.

MOVING TOWARD AN INTEGRATION

Assuming the legitimacy of both the commodity- and meaning-based views of the corporation, the single most important question about the future of business ethics is how to integrate these distinct views. The commodity-based view of the corporation is familiar and convenient. It often provides a way to divide up the economic pie in a noncontroversial manner. It allows men and women from different cultures, societies, and religions to engage in commerce with one another and to produce unprecedented wealth with a minimum of conflict. We come to work with the attitude "to each his own." In seeking profit, it's not so much that we ignore meaning but that no such category exists. As noted before, the great benefits of the commodity-based view should not be underestimated. The meaning-based view of the corporation, by contrast, insists, as James March noted, "The reason people involved in decision making devote so much time to symbols, myths, and rituals is that they care more about them" (1994, p. 218). We care about them, because we care about the meaning and significance of our decisions.

The position taken here is that a coherent integration of both views will have to start with the meaning-based view as prior and the commodity-based view as derivative. The point is that while it is possible to begin with a meaning-based view of the corporation and then subsequently carve out an appropriate and *limited* commodity-based view as part of a much larger vision, the reverse is impossible. This is true because a meaning-based view might quickly recognize its own limitations and exploit some of the benefits of a commodity-based view. It makes sense to say that a limited commodity-based view is appropriate because it is ultimately more meaningful. The reverse, however, is not true. It is impossible to start from a commodity-based view and entertain any thoughts of meaningful action. The commodity-based view simply has no vocabulary in which to communicate and express meaning. In other words, while the meaning-based view can encompass the commodity-based view, the commodity-based view cannot encompass the meaning-based view. Hence, the meaning-based view is axiomatic.

In practical terms, an implication for this observation is that an important and perhaps overriding task for business managers and others interested in these issues will be to help draw the appropriate boundaries between the meaning-based and the commodity-based views of the corporation. Under what specific conditions would a meaning-based view retreat in favor of the commodity-based view? Alternatively, when would the meaning-based view assert its priority over the commodity-based view? While no final answer is offered here, as we begin to take up the remaining six business ethics questions, it is useful to keep the distinction between the commodity- and meaning-based views on the front burner.

3

How Do
Ethical Decisions Happen?

Imagine for a moment that you are the chief executive officer (CEO) of PPL Therapeutics P.L.C., a small but up-and-coming Edinburgh biotechnology company. It is early 1997, and the following news story has just been publicly released. One of your hardworking scientists, Dr. Ian Wilmut, and his colleagues have successfully cloned a sheep (they named her after the singer/actress Dolly Parton), confounding the predictions of most of the world's top biologists. Your company has applied for patents on this technology, which involves taking udder cells from a six-year-old sheep, and you are confident the patents will be approved. The stock price has risen more than 16 percent on the news. As CEO, your company owns the technology that could change the world, and the world awaits your decision. Should your company continue to vigorously pursue "cloning" as a corporate strategy?

I suppose an extreme advocate of the commodity-based view might suggest leaving the ethical problems for government regulators to sort out, but such a solution seems to miss the crucial point of this story. This is certainly a business decision, but it's also a decision that will affect not only you as the CEO but how all of us think about life and its meanings.

over the pass. I took off after several of our porters who had gone ahead. (1990, p. 193)

After McCoy abruptly left, Stephen tried to convince Pasang to order some of the porters to carry the sadhu to a lower altitude, but Pasang resisted the idea, arguing that the porters would need all of their remaining strength to get over the pass themselves. Stephen also tried to convince the Japanese party to let him borrow their horse to transport the sadhu to a lower altitude, but the members of this party also refused. Stephen, in deep despair, finally left the sadhu lying on the ground listlessly throwing rocks at the Japanese group's dog. To this day, neither Stephen nor McCoy knows if the Indian holy man is alive or dead.

WHAT DOES THE PARABLE TEACH US?

McCoy's parable shares many characteristics with the classic business ethics dilemma. For this reason the case is worth studying extensively. As typically happens in business, problems, ethical or otherwise, arrive unexpectedly and require an immediate response. It is almost impossible to predict the arrival of a true ethical dilemma, and pushing off a decision is often impossible. Like the sadhu, ethical problems are "dumped" at our feet and require immediate attention.

Further, ethical problems in business often arise because of a lack of clarity as to precisely who within a group is responsible for a particular situation. For example, the Exxon *Valdez* disaster highlights a number of interesting questions as to who is responsible for corporate actions. Can managers and shareholders at Exxon simply argue that Captain Joseph Hazelwood, who was legally drunk when he was tested more than ten hours after the wreck, is solely responsible? To what extent is the third mate Gregory Cousins, the individual who actually steered the vessel onto the submerged rocks, culpable? Does the Coast Guard, which failed to detect the wandering ship, bear any responsibility? Corporate actions involve the cooperative effort of numerous individuals. Because of this it is often extremely difficult to assign ethical responsibility while the dilemma is being faced or even in retrospect. In the case of the sadhu, McCoy suggests that no one individual working alone could have saved him. An adequate solution required a group effort.

Third, as in business, McCoy and his fellow hikers were involved in pursuing a superordinate goal. The very purpose of their mission was universally perceived to be reaching the summit. In the business context, the superordinate goal is thought to be profit maximization. Ethical actions and solutions often require the group to postpone or lower previously sought goals, even where substantial investments of time and money in pursuit of the goal have already been incurred.

Finally, business dilemmas are ambiguous. Not only do they arrive unexpectedly, but when they do arrive, they bear no labels. As McCoy himself correctly notes, "Real moral dilemmas are ambiguous, and many of us hike right through them, unaware that they exist" (1990, p. 196).

McCoy and his fellow hikers, high on adrenaline and expectation, unexpectedly and inadvertently stumbled into an ethical dilemma. To be sure, at the time, the hikers failed to recognize it as such. The hikers' inability to adequately meet the needs of the helpless Indian holy man parallels many of today's modern business failures. The purpose of this chapter is to examine the causes for these breakdowns. Why do we fail at business ethics? How can we begin to "think ethically"? A plausible answer to these questions might help us to avoid future ethical traps and lays the groundwork for understanding the foundations of the meaning-based organization.

A PROBLEM OF "FRAMING"

The main point of this chapter is that many business ethics failures are caused by our inability to consider the logic of decision making. Most business curricula teach students to view decisions almost exclusively as opportunities to maximize self-interest. This is, of course, perfectly consistent with the commodity-based view of the organization, outlined in the preceding chapter. In many cases this strategy is well warranted. But, like any ideology, when taken to an extreme, the ideology of rational decision making can lead to perverse and undesirable results. Important business decisions can also be "framed" as ethical decisions. Consistent with the meaning-based view of the organization introduced in the preceding chapter, it makes sense to emphasize that decision making also provides opportunities to explore issues of identity and to seek personal and communal meaning. Although attempts have been made to show how ethical decision making is consistent with a pure logic of consequence, ultimately, the unique characteristics of these kinds of decisions do not easily fit into the dominant business ideology. Business decisions will finally be improved by understanding and examining the ambiguities associated with corporate decision making and searching for better ways to resolve them. Ethical dilemmas are never well defined and rarely well understood. Treating ethical dilemmas as "ordinary" decisions is often tantamount to ignoring them, and ignoring them inexorably leads to business ethics failures. The meaning-based organization must necessarily move beyond the exclusive use of the rational model of decision making.

THE USES AND LIMITS OF THE RATIONAL MODEL

The rational model of decision making is an extremely important tool for business managers. The recommendation discussed here in no way calls for the jettisoning of the rational model. Rather, the rational model needs to be viewed in its proper context. It is one tool of decision making among others.

The decision theorist James March, whose work I introduced in the preceding chapter, has provided a comprehensive description of the rational model. In March's view, standard theories of choice always assume decision processes are both *consequential* and *preference-based*. Actions, taken today, are dependent on the anticipated consequences of those actions. Decision processes are preference-based in the sense that anticipated consequences are always valued exclusively in terms of personal preferences. Alternative actions are judged in terms of the extent to which their expected future consequences are perceived to serve the preferences of the decision maker.

March (1994) efficiently summarizes his discussion of the rational model as follows:

A rational procedure is one that pursues a logic of consequence. It makes a choice conditional on the answers to four basic questions:

1. The question of *alternatives*: What actions are possible?

2. The question of *expectations*: What future consequences might follow from each alternative? How likely is each possible consequence, assuming that alternative is chosen?

3. The question of *preferences*: How valuable (to the decision maker) are the consequences associated with each of the alternatives?

4. The question of the *decision rule*: How is a choice to be made among the alternatives in terms of the values of the consequences? (pp. 2–3)

There can be no debate that careful, systematic, and thorough attention to these four questions has improved and will continue to improve the efficiency of decision making.

Examples of improved decision making in business as a result of a better and more thorough application of the rational model abound. Investors interested in maximizing their returns have been served well by insights gleaned from portfolio theory. Money managers depend heavily on the concept of the time value of money. Corporate managers contemplating new investments have succeeded by applying notions of cost-benefit analysis and capital budgeting. Marketing experts have improved their techniques by applying sophisticated statistical tools. Although this list could be multiplied easily, it is really not necessary.

With such successes in mind, one might even be tempted to argue that in McCoy's ethical conflict the decision outcome could have been improved by a more self-conscious use of the rational model. Thorough-going proponents of the rational decision-making model would propose, perhaps, that the failure here, if indeed there is a failure, is not too much rationality but too little.

First, McCoy did not carefully identify all possible alternatives. An intended rational strategy requires decision makers to consider the full set of available options. McCoy's self-report, taken at face value, suggests that at the moment of decision, he never considered the option of forgoing the climb in order to help Stephen carry the sadhu down to safety.

Second, it is clear from McCoy's description that he initially did not consider the connection between his decision to continue the climb and the ultimate well-being of the Indian holy man. McCoy is apparently taken by surprise when Stephen finally joined him at the summit. McCoy writes, "Still exhilarated by victory, I ran down the slope to congratulate him [Stephen]. He was suffering from altitude sickness, walking fifteen steps, then stopping, walking fifteen steps, then stopping. Pasang accompanied him all the way up. When I reached them, Stephen glared at me and said: 'How do you feel about contributing to the death of a fellow man?'" (1990, p. 193). The "exhilarated" McCoy was genuinely surprised by the question.

Third and perhaps most important, preferences were not systematically examined. Throughout the ordeal and even immediately afterward, McCoy takes as self-evident that climbing the mountain is the "apex of one of the most powerful experiences" (1990, p. 195) of his life. The possibility that saving the life of a desperately helpless human being—last seen lying on the ground listlessly throwing rocks at a dog—might also have proved to be an even more powerful experience was never seriously contemplated.

Proponents of the rational argument, assuming they would acknowledge that an ethical failure occurred, might want to conclude, then, that McCoy simply failed to act rationally in the strict sense that we are employing the term here. McCoy, if better trained as a rational decision maker and perhaps absent the intense physical pressures of the ordeal, would have carefully contemplated the available options and realized that his own self-interest, his own real preferences dictated abandoning the climb and saving the sadhu. Proponents of the rational argument might suggest that he really preferred saving the man's life but was not consciously aware of this at the moment of decision. If this diagnosis is correct, the solution is more rationality, not less.

Conceding the importance of this argument (there is a kernel of truth here), the final conclusion is dubious. A more plausible interpretation of McCoy's report suggests that at the very moment of decision, McCoy was indeed acting rationally, if by acting rationally we merely mean he was promoting his own perceived interests—as he perceived them at that moment. He might very well have considered all his options and their possible ramifications. Nevertheless, at the moment of decision, McCoy's preference for reaching the summit overwhelmed his desire to help the sadhu. The immediate prospect of successfully achieving a long-sought goal simply dwarfed the perceived personal benefits associated with the uncertain prospect of saving the sadhu.

Most of us, with a little self-reflection, can call to mind incidents where we pursued some activity that provided momentary satisfaction but that we "knew," even at the decisive moment, was not the "correct" course of action. Psychologists have noted that there is a tendency for immediate rewards to appear misleadingly attractive. Immediate rewards flood one's conscience and overwhelm one's judgments. This problem has been called the weak-will problem. Robert Frank expands:

When a pigeon is given a chance to peck one of two buttons to choose between a morsel of food 30 seconds from now and a much larger morsel 40 seconds from now, it takes the latter. But when it chooses between the same morsel now and the larger morsel 10 seconds hence, it often picks the former. Rats behave the same way. So do cats, dogs, guinea pigs, and hogs. And so, much of the time, do humans. This feature is apparently part of the hard-wiring of most animal nervous systems. (1988, p. 80)

Individuals with dangerously high levels of cholesterol know that eating foods high in saturated fats will increase their risk of a heart attack, yet they continue to consume red meats and cheeses. All of us are aware of the risks associated with cigarettes, yet smoking persists. In business, creators of Ponzi schemes surely must know that ultimately the strategy is self-defeating, yet, in the excitement of discovery, the lure of magnificent gains often makes Ponzi schemes too difficult to resist. The view propounded here suggests that, technically speaking, at the moment of decision, each of the "failures" just discussed, both at the level of the individual and at the level of the organization, reflects behavior consistent with canons of rationality; that is, in each case, decision makers are promoting perceived self-interest. As Frank further notes, "Given the nature of our psychological reward mechanism, a person who is purely self-interested will sometimes give in to his temptation to cheat, even when he knows cheating does not pay" (1988, p. 88; see also Nozick, 1993, for a different interpretation, especially pp. 14–21).

AN ALTERNATIVE VISION: THE LOGIC OF APPROPRIATENESS

The problem that Frank and others (see Ainslie, 1985) have identified is that our preferences are often structured such that the prospect of immediate gratification overwhelms our more permanent, long-run interests. Somewhat paradoxically, one solution to the weak-will problem is to abandon self-interest in favor of an alternative vision of human behavior. It is paradoxical because by abandoning pure rationality, ultimately, long-run interests are often promoted. James March has labeled this alternative vision the logic of appropriateness. According to March, the logic of appropriateness, like the rational model, can be summarized by a set of questions:

Decision makers are imagined to ask (explicitly or implicitly) three questions:
1. The question of *recognition*: What kind of situation is this?
2. The question of *identity*. What kind of a person am I? Or what kind of organization is this?
3. The question of *rules*: What does a person such as I, or an organization such as this, do in a situation such as this? (1994, p. 58)

The essence of the logic of appropriateness is the notion that decision making is ultimately not only about promoting one's immediate self-interest but is better envisaged as understanding, interpreting, and accepting ethical principles or rules of behavior. This perspective asserts that it is meaningful to talk about behavior as if behavior is meaningful (independent of personal preferences). As March himself makes explicit, "Decision makers can violate a logic of consequence and be considered stupid or naive, but if they violate the moral obligations of identity, they will be considered lacking in elementary virtue" (1994, p. 65).

To be sure, a logic of appropriateness recognizes that some behavior is dictated by individual self-interest, but the domain where self-interest commands jurisdiction is ultimately bounded by rules of appropriateness.

As Amitai Etzioni has perceptively noted, "The neoclassical paradigm (the rational model) is too simple: it does not include a pivotal distinction between the sense of pleasure—derived from consumption of goods and services, and from other sources—and the sense of affirmation attained when a person abides by his or her moral commitments" (1988, p. 36). Further, Etzioni asserts that casual empirical observation "shows that individuals who seek to live up to their moral commitments behave in a manner that is systematically and significantly different from those who act to enhance their pleasures" (1988, p. 67).

The paradoxical benefit of principled behavior is that it can serve as a mechanism for avoiding the weak-will problem. For example, diligent and honest businesspersons, tempted by the prospects of the immediate gains of a Ponzi scheme, might do well to remind themselves—at the moment of decision—of their principle that they are entitled to a profit only after producing a product or service with positive "social value." With the aid of a deeply held principle, even the most narrow, self-interested calculus might now call for forgoing the Ponzi scheme. The principled businessperson might reason as follows: "Although I attach a very high preference for immediate material rewards like money, the equally immediate sense of accomplishment (or affirmation) I will feel as a result of honoring my principle, coupled with the expected guilt I will feel if I break my principle, is more than sufficient to prevent me from participating in the Ponzi scheme." Careful notice and special emphasis should be given to the fact that the principle must be accepted for its own sake (i.e., it must give rise to true feelings of accomplishment or guilt) and cannot simply be invoked as a "trick" to avoid temptation. In other words, the principle must be considered meaningful to the decision maker.

Perhaps, the real decision McCoy and his fellow hikers faced was not how best to promote their own self-interest but whether or not the rational model was *appropriate* as the dominant mode of decision making. In other words, McCoy failed because he viewed his decision purely in terms of self-interest. The decision was framed as simply one more opportunity to promote individual preferences. Had McCoy chosen an alternative frame—what we are calling a logic of appropriateness—the decision outcome might have been improved.

Let us suppose McCoy had taken the ethically significant act of framing his choice in terms of the logic of appropriateness. Unlike the angry New Zealander, who peremptorily turned and went back up the mountain to join his friends, McCoy would have stepped outside himself and asked March's first question, "What kind of a situation is this?" Arguably, in this instance, the mere asking of this question would have been sufficient. Had McCoy been able to admit to himself, at the moment of decision, that continuing the climb would contribute (even if indirectly) to the death of the sadhu, it is highly unlikely that he would have chosen as he did. Stephen's question to McCoy is pertinent in this context. At the summit, he asks the following rhetorical question:

I wonder what the Sherpas would have done if the sadhu had been a well-dressed Nepali, or what the Japanese would have done if the sadhu had been a well-dressed Asian, or what you would have done, Buzz, if the sadhu had been a well-dressed Western woman? (1990, p. 195)

Stephen's question drives home the point that a human being's life was hanging in the balance. In the dilemma described here, nationality, wealth, and mode of dress are obviously not relevant factors. Being able to see through these externals, even in the heat of the moment, is an important first step in describing and resolving true ethical dilemmas.

Important as March's first question is, the second and third questions reflect the essence of the logic of appropriateness and distinguish it as an alternative mode of decision making. "What kind of person am I?" This question subsumes the question of preferences, which is at the foundation of the rational model. Here, however, not only does one ask how a given action will promote current preferences, but one is enjoined to question those very preferences. This question and March's third question, "What does a person such as I, or an organization such as this, do in a situation such as this?" invite and encourage the decision maker to utilize ethical criteria. The ability to critique one's own preferences (assumed in the second question) and alter them (assumed in the third question) is the heart and soul of the logic of appropriateness. Herein lies the major distinction between a purely rational model and the logic of appropriateness.

By contrast, the rational model always take preferences as completely stable and exogenous. "Preferences are assumed not to change substantially over time, not to be very different between wealthy and poor persons, or even between persons in different societies and cultures" (Becker, 1976, p. 5; see also Stigler and Becker, 1977). The assumption underlying this view is that tastes will be unchanged even when the outcomes of actions taken today are realized (March, 1978). Further, standard theories of choice assume that tastes are absolute. "Normative theories of choice assume a formal posture of moral relativism. The theories insist on morality of action in terms of tastes; but they recognize neither discriminations among alternative tastes, nor the possibility that a person reasonably might view his own preferences and actions based on them as morally distressing" (March, 1978, p. 595). Advocates of the rational model ignore the effects of education, art, literature, community, religious beliefs, persuasion, and the role of leadership. Etzioni criticizes this view. He writes that it is "as if economic man was a biological-psychological miracle born fully formed, say in his mid-twenties with his preferences 'immaculately conceived' as Kenneth Boulding put it to a 1985 George Washington University Seminar on socio-economics" (Etzioni, 1988, p. 10).

After the fact, commenting on his own behavior, McCoy himself seemingly recognizes the failure of the rational model and, in turn, his own personal failure in this instance. The tremendous depth and power of *The Parable of the Sadhu* derive, in large measure, from McCoy's vulnerable, honest, and perceptive self-criticism, which ultimately leads him to embrace a logic of appropriateness:

What would have happened had Stephen and I carried the sadhu for two days back to the village and become involved with the villagers in his care? In four trips to Nepal my most interesting experiences occurred in 1975 when I lived in a Sherpa home in the Khumbu for five days recovering from altitude sickness. The high point of Stephen's trip was an invitation to participate in a family funeral ceremony in Manang. Neither experience had to do with climbing the high passes of the Himalayas. Why were we so reluctant to try the lower path, the ambiguous trail? (1990, p. 199)

McCoy's final conclusion is unintelligible from a purely rational approach. His language is the language of appropriateness rather than self-interest. Focusing specifically on business ethics, he anticipates March's second and third questions when he finally concludes, "What is the nature of our responsibility if we consider ourselves to be ethical persons? Perhaps it is to change the values of the group so that it can, with all its resources, take the other road" (1990, p. 200).

PUTTING THE MODEL OF APPROPRIATENESS TO WORK

This chapter suggests that creating and sustaining effective, meaning-based organizations imply two specific and practical recommendations:

1. Individuals will have to learn to view decision making not only in terms of the rational model but also in terms of the model of appropriateness.
2. Organizations will have to be structured in such a way as to "allow" individuals enough freedom to pursue the first recommendation.

I am not suggesting that all decisions will be framed in terms of the model of appropriateness. Efficiency probably requires that the vast majority of decisions will, in fact, be considered using the apparatus of the rational model. Nevertheless, the most significant business decisions require recourse to a more subtle method of decision making. As individuals, we must learn to be more self-conscious about decision making. Did I consider this decision only from the perspective of the rational model? Or did I ask what a person like me "should" do in situation like this?

This perspective asserts that business leaders are often like contemporary doctors who are faced with the excruciatingly difficult question of assisted suicide. While no easy answers suggest themselves, there is little doubt that this issue requires recourse to the model of appropriateness. What does it *mean* to be a doctor? Can mechanical procedures be set up in such a way to ensure that assisted suicide is a legitimate medical technique and not just the work of a rogue medical professional? So, too, accountants, aware of managerial misdeeds, must ask, What does it mean to be an accountant? Or marketers, asked to prepare cigarette promotions designed to increase smoking among children, must ask, What does it mean to be an advertiser?

Important as it is, the first recommendation without the second is hardly complete. Ernest Hemingway's beguiling and simple novel *The Old Man and the Sea* paints a melancholy picture of the proud, but solitary, man in search of the big, but somewhat mysterious, fish. As one dreamily reads this novel, it is almost impossible not to begin rooting for the old fisherman on his quest, as it slowly dawns on the reader that the elusive fish is the old man's "meaning." Battling with the fish and working alone for days out on the great sea, the old man finally does catch the immense marlin, only to have it eaten by sharks before he can reach shore and enjoy his bounty. The old man is not as disappointed as this brief summary might suggest. Perhaps, Hemingway and his protagonist are here to remind us that the search for meaning is ultimately never completely successful. Hemingway's old man, however, provides a poor symbol for the business manager who wants to take ethics seriously. Business leaders, embedded in organizational and communal life, are *not* like the lonely fisherman of this novel. It is interesting that Hemingway chose the sports metaphor of fishing to stand for man's search for meaning. Fishing is one of the few sports engaged in as an individual. Business ethics emphasizes that in our search for meaning we are more like members of a basketball or soccer team than the old man and the sea.

Because business is a team sport, the best organizational leaders, accustomed to a meaning-based perspective, necessarily ask, Is the organization structured in such a way as to encourage (and reward) advocates of the model of appropriateness? This question subsumes two separate issues: authority and accountability. Are "experts" in the organization given the authority to impact those decisions that require their specific expertise? Are those responsible for decision making ultimately held accountable for their decisions? The notion of a meaning-based organization is itself meaningless (or worse) unless it is consciously designed and supported as such by top management.

It is almost easier to understand what an effective, meaning-based organization looks like by examining its opposite. On March 28, 1986, the National Aeronautics and Space Administration (NASA), with the explicit approval of a major parts supplier, Morton Thiokol, launched the ill-fated *Challenger* space shuttle. Moments later, following a horrific explosion, the astronauts died as their capsule hurled out of the sky toward the ocean at about 200 miles per hour. This happened in spite of the fact that engineers at Morton Thiokol had unanimously warned of just such a possibility, according to a revealing report written by Roger Boisjoly, an engineer at Thiokol at the time and self-described as "the engineer most knowledgeable about the Space Shuttle Booster Joints" (1993, p. 61). His revelations provide a remarkably stark reminder of what can happen when the wrong decision model is employed at the organizational level.

After already experiencing a near-tragedy at 53 degrees Fahrenheit, engineers at Thiokol were apprehensive about launching the *Challenger* in cold weather. The problem, as the engineers understood it (and as Boisjoly explained it after the fact), was whether or not the O-rings would seal at low temperatures. Preliminary test data suggested that the O-rings would have great difficultly sealing at temperatures below 50 degrees. If these rings did not seal properly, an explosion of the sort that actually occurred could not be ruled out. Based on these considerations, engineers recommended the conservative decision rule: do not launch the Challenger below temperatures of 53 degrees.

NASA was not happy with this decision. The opinion of Larry Mulloy at the Kennedy Space Center was that "the technical data presented was 'inconclusive' and didn't support stopping the launch. He also made a statement to Morton Thiokol management stating, 'My God, Thiokol, when do you want me to launch, next April?' His summary and statements further escalated the pressure on Morton Thiokol management to launch" (Boisjoly, 1993 p. 61). In response to this statement by Mulloy, management, in fact, did reconsider its earlier recommendation.

Morton Thiokol's general manager and three vice presidents privately discussed the situation. What was to be a five-minute caucus turned into a 30-minute meeting. Most tellingly for present purposes:

Just before the vote was taken by the managers, the General Manager told the VP of engineering to *"Take off your engineering hat and put on your management hat."* The vote was then immediately taken and it was four positive votes for launch. No engineer in the room was allowed to vote or participate in the discussion which formulated the rationale for a launch decision. (Boisjoly, p. 63)

"Take off your engineering hat and put on your management hat." Roughly translated into the language introduced in this chapter: "Use the rational model and not the model of appropriateness." The great irony, of course, is that, ultimately, the use of the model of appropriateness would have generated a decision outcome far superior, even if viewed from the rational model perspective. Perhaps the most tragic aspect of Challenger catastrophe is that it might very well have been avoided by a more self-conscious understanding of how organizational decisions happen.

THE IMPORTANCE OF STRUCTURE

How important are organizational structure and design to business ethics? Maybe Morton Thiokol is the exception and not the rule. After all, it is often asserted that we learn ethics at home and only at home. By the time students enter college it is too late in the game to introduce ethics into the curriculum, or so the argument goes. There might be some truth to these observations if ethics was only about what the solitary individual does in his or her spare time. But, as we have observed, business is a team sport. One reason that organization design is so important, perhaps of paramount importance to business ethics, is the simple, but regularly observable, fact that human beings tend to do what they are told to do, especially when the authority figure is somehow perceived as "legitimate" in their eyes.

No one has demonstrated this proposition more forcefully and carefully than the social psychologist Stanley Milgram. Deeply troubled by the thought that large numbers of German citizens willingly participated and allowed the Nazi Holocaust to happen, Milgram set out to study what he called "obedience to authority" (1974).

Milgram asked volunteers in the New Haven, Connecticut, area to participate in what he described to them in a public advertisement as a learning experiment. What the participants did not know was that, as part of the experiment, they would be asked to carry out a series of acts that would come increasingly in conflict with conscience. "The main question is how far the participant will comply with the experimenter's instructions before refusing to carry out the actions required of him" (1974, p. 3).

The specifics of the laboratory experiment are as follows. Two people come to the laboratory to participate in the learning experiment. One is called the "teacher," and the other is called the "learner." They are told that the point of the experiment is to understand how punishment affects learning. The "learner" is strapped into a chair and is attached to an electrode. He is to learn a list of word pairs. If at any point, he makes a mistake, the "teacher," who is seated in another room in front of an impressive shock generator, will give him electric shocks of increasing intensity. The machine itself carries clear warnings about the dangers of severe shocks.

The real focus of the experiment is the "teacher." In fact, the "learner" is an actor working with the experimenter. He purposely does not learn the words correctly. He is instructed to grunt at low-level shocks (75 volts), to complain verbally at higher levels (125 volts), to demand to be released at still higher levels (150 volts), and to agonizingly scream at the highest level (285 volts). The point is to see how far the "teacher," who is the only genuinely naive subject in this experiment, will go. In reality, of course, no shocks are being administered. If at any point during the experiment the "teacher" hesitates, the experimenter orders him to continue. The experiment is over only when the "teacher" physically gets up and leaves the room.

The results are consistent and dramatic:

Many subjects will obey the experimenter no matter how vehement the pleading of the person being shocked, no matter how painful the shocks seem to be, and no matter how much the victim pleads to be let out. This was seen time and again in our studies and has been observed in several universities where the experiment was repeated. It is the extreme willingness of adults to go to almost any lengths on the command of an authority that constitutes the chief finding of the study and the fact most urgently demanding explanation. (Milgram, 1974, p. 5)

The question of why subjects are so obedient is not easy to answer, especially when we consider the fact that these same subjects reportedly felt, even while they were participating in the experiments, that their actions were incompatible with their own notions of morality. Milgram offers the following possibilities. Subjects want to be polite and maintain a cordial relationship with the experimenter. Subjects become focused on the technical aspect of the job and push aside moral considerations. They don't see themselves as responsible for their actions, reasoning that the experimenter is in charge. They treat the experiment as if it simply has to be carried out, forgetting that it was originally devised by a human being who, at minimum, needs to be able to provide a compelling rationale for inflicting harm on the "learner." The laboratory has a strong claim to legitimacy. If it's being carried out here at the university, it must be OK. Finally, Milgram concludes, "The form and shape of society and the way it is developing have much to do with it . . . the breaking up of society into people carrying out narrow and very special jobs takes away from the human quality of work and life. A person does not get to see the whole situation but only a small part of it, and is thus unable to act without some kind of over-all direction. He yields to authority but in doing so is alienated from his own actions" (1974, p. 11).

But even as he is diagnosing and explaining the causes of the problem, Milgram provides the seeds for its solution (or, at least, partial solution). If human beings have this tendency to do what they are told to do, we have to turn our attention to the "form and shape of society." For the business manager, this means the structure of the business organization.

As the Morton Thiokol case and Stanley Milgram's famous psychological experiment demonstrate, effective, meaning-based organizations will have to be designed and built in such a way as to "allow" individuals enough freedom to pursue vigorously and unabashedly the model of appropriateness. If decision making in an organization is only about promoting one's own preconceived interests or even the organization's narrow interests, the organization is in more trouble than it knows. Organizations need articulated visions, formal codes of conduct, quality control, ombudsmen, and reward mechanisms that promote human meaning.

Neither of the two recommendations offered at the beginning of the previous section is offered as a cure-all. The two recommendations merely mark the starting point and a direction to follow as we begin a substantive discussion of business ethics.

CONCLUSION

Unabashedly introducing meaning into the business ethics equation is meant to be purposely provocative. It opens up a dimension of life that some would prefer to keep sealed off. Talking about meaning makes us vulnerable, and, to many, mixing the metaphors of business and meaning creates a shrill poem. For these people meaning may have its place, but its place is not the company board room or managerial offices.

I end this chapter with a prediction and an additional question. Corporations will be understood as "symbols," not just tools. But what will they come to symbolize?

The famous theologian Paul Tillich once described the difference between signs and symbols as follows: while both the sign and symbol "point beyond themselves to something else" (1957, p. 41), only the symbol "participates in that to which it points" (1957, p. 42). A stoplight is merely a sign, but a flag is a symbol. According to this distinction, corporations are surely symbols. But symbols of what?

James March, in exploring the rich language and varied rituals associated with decision making in the modern corporation, suggests one possible answer:

The processes of choice reassure those involved that the choice has been made intelligently; that it reflects planning, thinking, analysis, and the systematic use of information; that people have acted appropriately as decision makers; that the choice is sensitive to the concerns of relevant people; and that the right people are involved. At the same time, the processes of choice reassure those involved of their own significance. In particular, the processes are used to reinforce the idea that decision makers and their decisions affect the course of history, and do so properly. (1994, p. 217)

In short, March suggests that the rituals of decision making symbolize our deep attachment to the rational pursuit of human interests. In March's writings this becomes an exciting, encouraging, and seemingly accessible proposition.

Maybe we should end this chapter here; nevertheless, I am prodded on and tempted to suggest that corporations might eventually come to symbolize even more. The Jewish Talmud offers the following trenchant criticism of the Roman empire:

In times to come, God will take a scroll of the Law in His embrace and proclaim: "Let him who has occupied himself with the Torah, come and take his reward." ... the Kingdom Rome will enter first before Him ... God will then say to them: "How have you occupied yourselves?" They will reply: ... "we have established many marketplaces, we have erected many baths, we have accumulated much gold and silver, and all this we did only for the sake of ... Torah." God will say in reply: "You foolish ones among peoples, all that which you have done, you have only done to satisfy your own desires. You have established marketplaces to place courtesans therein; baths to revel in them; [as to the accumulation of] silver and gold that is Mine, as it is written: Mine is the silver and Mine is the gold, saith the Lord of Hosts." (Talmudic Tractate: Avodah Zarah: 2B)

As this hypothetical conversation illustrates, the satisfaction of desires alone is not a sufficient justification for engaging in economic activities. The author of this rabbinic parable understood the importance and necessity for "marketplaces," "baths," "gold," and "silver." He does not suggest that engaging in "secular" activities is inappropriate. Rather, the point is that economic activities are never to be viewed only as ends in themselves. Economic activities—at the individual, organizational, and national level—are a means toward building a just and caring society in which the best of human and spiritual values might flourish. Might corporations, someday, also come to symbolize an attachment to human meaning?

4

How Fair Is Fair?

One of the most primitive building blocks of business ethics is the notion of fairness. From the very young to the very old, all of us want to be treated in a fair way. While fairness is not the be-all and end-all of business ethics, it is a necessary first step. But, at this point in the discussion, it is useful to step back and ask, How fair is fair? With some good answers to this question, the business ethics conversation is sharpened and becomes more useful.

Economists usually assume firms behave as if they maximize profits subject only to legal and budgetary constraints. For many purposes this core assumption of economics provides interesting, useful, and important results. Nevertheless, it is often an incomplete description of firm behavior. Ironically, those firms that adopt the economists' description as a prescriptive mandate may actually perform worse than other firms (Pava and Krausz, 1996).

Kahneman, Knetsch, and Thaler (1986; hereafter, KKT) have provided persuasive survey evidence suggesting that maximizing firms also consider "fairness" constraints. Following Akerlof (1979), Solow (1980), and Okun (1981), the authors suggest that fairness constraints explain why many markets fail to clear in the short run and why suppliers often describe a cut in price as a "discount" rather than as a reduction in the list price. The authors claim no necessary normative status for fairness constraints. Rather, fairness is treated as a kind of community norm and is defined operationally as "a substantial majority of the population studied thinks it's fair" (KKT, 1986, p. 729).

To document the existence of fairness constraints, KKT presented a number of short business scenarios to a random sample of Canadian residents and asked respondents to rate the scenarios as very unfair, unfair, acceptable, or completely fair. For example, the authors asked respondents to rate the following scenario:

A hardware store has been selling snow shovels for $15. The morning after a large snowstorm, the store raises the price to $20. (p. 728)

The vast majority of respondents, 82 percent, rated this decision as either completely unfair or unfair. Only 18 percent rated the action as acceptable or completely fair. In this scenario, the hardware store is attempting to capture profits in response to an exogenous increase in demand spurred on by the unpredictable snowstorm. Apparently, most respondents view such profits, resulting from the mere transfer of wealth from customers to the firm, as tainted in some way. Not all profits are alike. From a purely free market perspective—with no vocabulary to describe community norms of fairness—such results are difficult, if not impossible, to interpret.

SIMPLE FAIRNESS

KKT suggest that this scenario and others provide strong evidence for the following formal proposition: "The cardinal rule of fair behavior is surely that one person should not achieve a gain by simply imposing an *equivalent* loss on another" (p. 731; emphasis added). We refer to this proposition as *simple fairness*. In the snow shovel example, the five-dollar gain to the firm is taken directly from the representative customer, who now pays the additional five dollars. The firm itself has nothing to do with the snowstorm, and its own costs are unaffected. Had the price increase been justified as a result of this increase in wholesale prices (or even a relatively smaller increase), respondents would be much less likely to rate the firm's action as unfair. In this alternative formulation of the scenario, the firm itself is not profiting, and therefore there is no violation of *simple fairness*.

The proposition is labeled here as simple for two reasons: (1) it applies across a wide spectrum of diverse situations, and (2) at least theoretically, it is straightforward to use. If A has knowledge of the loss he or she is imposing on B, A must forgo the equivalent profit. This proposition suggests the existence of a bright line dividing fair and unfair behavior. In KKT's words, "Transactors have an entitlement to the terms of the reference transaction and firms are entitled to their reference profit. A firm is not allowed to increase its profits by arbitrarily violating the entitlement of its transactors to the reference price, rent, or wage" (p. 729). In the case at hand, the reference profit is the profit earned in the absence of the snowstorm, and the reference price is the original price of the snow shovels.

Two caveats are in order here. First, although it is true that the proposition holds across a wide spectrum of diverse situations, it is by no means universal. Consider, for example, the following scenario:

A small company employs several workers and has been paying them average wages. There is severe unemployment in the area and the company could easily replace its current workers with good workers at a lower wage. The company has been losing money. The owners reduce the current workers' wages by 5 percent. (KKT, 1986, p. 733)

Almost 70 percent of respondents rated this behavior as acceptable or better, and only about 30 percent perceived this as unfair. Apparently, what makes this scenario unique is the additional fact that the company has been losing money. In fact, when the otherwise identical scenario reads, "The company has been making money," more than 75 percent of respondents rate it as unfair. Second, even if, theoretically, the use of this proposition is straightforward, in practice it is often difficult to apply. Unlike the snow shovel example, in many real-life situations business decision makers simply don't know the precise dollar amount of losses imposed on customers, employees, and others. In spite of these limitations, the notion of simple fairness is useful and ubiquitous.

SIMPLE FAIRNESS VERSUS COMPLEX FAIRNESS

Simple fairness is not restricted to customer markets but holds in employer and employee relationships and in landlord and tenant relationships, as well. For example, 83 percent of respondents rated the following scenario either unfair or completely unfair:

A small photocopying shop has one employee who has worked in the shop for six months and earns $9 per hour. Business continues to be satisfactory, but a factory in the area has closed and unemployment has increased. Other small shops have now hired reliable workers at $7 an hour to perform jobs similar to those done by the photocopy shop employee. The owner of the photocopying shop reduces the employee's wage to $7. (KKT, p. 730)

Similarly, more than 90 percent of respondents rated the following scenario from the real estate industry as unfair or completely unfair:

A landlord rents out a small house. When the lease is due for renewal, the landlord learns that the tenant has taken a job very close to the house and is therefore unlikely to move. The landlord raises the rent $40 per month more than he was planning to do. (KKT, p. 730)

As in the snow shovel example, these two cases represent merely a transfer of wealth from one party to another. In the photocopying example, the firm captures the full benefit of the employee's two-dollar an hour loss, and in the landlord case the landlord keeps the extra $40 per month that the tenant must now pay. Both of these cases clearly violate the proposition that one person should not achieve a gain by simply imposing an equivalent loss on another.

The existence of community norms of fairness in a wide variety of economic settings, as documented by KKT, suggests an interesting follow-up question. If simple fairness serves as a constraint or a potential constraint on profit-maximizing behavior, would an even more restrictive rule of fairness govern at least some economic transactions?

This chapter extends the KKT paper by examining the following, more restrictive proposition, which we label *complex fairness*: one person should not achieve a relatively large gain by imposing a relatively small loss on another.

This proposition suggests that under certain, carefully prescribed circumstances fairness constraints will cause firms not only to forgo a profit when an equivalent loss is imposed on another party, but to forgo relatively large profits when a relatively small loss is imposed on another party. We label this as complex fairness for two distinct reasons. (1) To a far greater degree than simple fairness, we expect this proposition to be highly dependent on context. It is unlikely that complex fairness applies across the board to the same extent that simple fairness does. More specifically, we expect this proposition to hold primarily in those situations where A is clearly superior to B in some relevant characteristic, especially wealth. (2) This proposition is ambiguous and more difficult to use than the first proposition. Here, there is no bright line that naturally divides fair and unfair behavior. Managers, on a case-by-case basis, need to judge the meaning of "a relatively large gain" and "a relatively small loss." Easily discernible and noncontroversial "reference profits" and "reference prices" are difficult to discover and apply.

STATING THE QUESTION AND A WAY TO ANSWER IT

The specific questions of this chapter can now be succinctly stated as follows. Is complex fairness ever a community standard? If so, how large is a "relatively large gain," and how small is "a relatively small loss"? To answer these questions, we administered the following questionnaire (it includes two cases) to 101 business student respondents. All respondents had some exposure to time-value concepts. These scenarios, reproduced in full, are hypothetical cases designed to capture a realistic and pervasive problem in the real estate industry. In virtually all rehab projects managers choose whether or not to factor in costs imposed on non-contracting third parties. The hypothetical example that follows is purposely exaggerated in order to highlight the underlying ethical dilemma, but the essence of the choice is retained.

Real Estate Scenarios: Case 1

You are managing a residential apartment complex in a small, aging, industrial town on the Massachusetts and Vermont border. Your company (of which you are a 10% partner) paid $1,000,000 cash for the complex which consists of 100 separate housing units. The apartments require repairs. You are asked to choose between the following two rehabilitation projects:

Project A—Complete "Rehab"

The company incurs an additional $1,000,000 of costs to repair and modernize the apartment complex. Repairs are made both externally and internally. After completion of the rehab (approximately 1 year), rents will be raised for each of the 100 housing units from $4,000 per year (current rental rates) to $5,000 per year. You are certain occupancy will be 100% for all future periods. Prevailing interest rates are 5%. (*Hint*: The present value of a perpetuity [an annuity of infinite length] is equal to the rent divided by the interest rate [in this case 5%].)

Project B—Partial "Rehab"

The company incurs an additional $250,000 of costs to repair and modernize the apartment complex. Repairs are made both externally and internally, but are generally cosmetic changes. After completion of the rehab (approximately 1 year), rents will be raised for each of the housing units from $4,000 per year (current rental rates) to $4,250 per year. You are certain occupancy will be 100% for the foreseeable future. Prevailing interest rates are 5%. (*Hint*: The present value of a perpetuity [an annuity of infinite length] is equal to the rent divided by the interest rate [in this case 5 percent].)

Required: Assuming you must choose either PROJECT A or PROJECT B, which would you choose? Circle one:

Project A   Project B

If you selected Project B, ——— stop here.

Case 2

This case is the same as above, except if you choose Project A, the 100 current tenants will not be able to afford the new, higher rents. Each of the 100 tenants will incur a relocation fee of $15,000.

A—*Required*: Assuming you must choose either Project A or Project B, which would you choose? Circle one:

Project A   Project B

If you selected Project A, ——— stop here.

B—*Required*: If you are still participating in this experiment, in the absence of any relocation fees you selected Project A, and with a $15,000 relocation fee you switched your answer to Project B. Choose any dollar amount between $1 and $14,999 for the relocation fee which would cause you to be indifferent between Project A and Project B. Write in the amount here $———.

Case 1 is straightforward and is included as a device to screen out non-profit-maximizing respondents.[1] Respondents are expected to compare the net present values of Projects A and B. In the absence of any external costs, rational respondents will choose the project that yields the highest net present value. Since the choice is between Projects A and B only, rational investors focus only on the "additional revenues" and the "additional costs" to determine the net present values. In this case, the real estate company raises rents $1,000 per unit times the 100 separate housing units, or $100,000 in total. For simplicity, the case assumes that occupancy will be 100 percent for all future periods. The present value of the additional revenues is therefore $2 million ($100,000 divided by the assumed interest rate of 5 percent). If we subtract the additional $1 million of costs needed to repair and modernize the apartment for the complete rehab, we are left with a net present value of $1 million for Project A. The net present value for Project B, described as a partial rehab, can be calculated using the exact same procedure. The net present value for Project B is $250,000. Thus, Project A, the full rehab, is the profit-maximizing choice. Project A is $750,000 more valuable than Project B. Not unexpectedly, the vast majority of our sample, made up entirely of accounting students with at least some exposure to present value concepts, chose Project A. In fact, nearly 80 percent (80 out of 101) chose the profit-maximizing alternative.

These 80 respondents, the profit-maximizing respondents, were then asked to consider Case 2. Case 2 is identical to Case 1 in all respects except one. The 100 current tenants each incurs a relocation fee of $15,000, as they can no longer "afford the new, higher rents." Importantly, occupancy is still assumed to be 100 percent for all future periods. More than 71 percent of respondents (statistically significant) switched from Project A to Project B. This result indicates that even profit maximizers factor in external costs when those external costs are relatively high. This result is consistent with those results obtained by KKT discussed earlier and is expected in a community that, at minimum, accepts some notion of simple fairness. In this case, we describe the $15,000 relocation fee, or the total relocation fee of $1,500,000, as relatively high because it is twice the difference between the net present values of Projects A and B. In other words, respondents who choose Project A, in Case 1, and Project B, in Case 2, are forgoing a profit of $750,000 in order to avoid imposing a total cost of $1,500,000 on current tenants. Remember, if simple fairness holds, it suggests that one person should not achieve a gain by imposing an equivalent loss on another. This certainly implies that one person should not achieve a gain of $x by imposing a loss of 2 times $x on another party, as is the case here.

Requirement B in Case 2 is an attempt to formally distinguish between simple and complex fairness. Requirement B reads, "If you are still participating in this experiment, in the absence of any relocation fees you selected PROJECT A, and with a $15,000 relocation fee you switched your answer to PROJECT B." It asks respondents to choose any dollar amount between $1 and $14,999 as the relocation fee that would cause them to be indifferent between Projects A and B. The mean response was $5,316 (statistically smaller than $7,500). The accompanying table shows the results.

Statistical Summary of Responses to Case 2

Mean Response	$5,316
Median Response	$5,000
Standard Error	$571
Z-Statistic	3.82
Probability Level	.02

We consider $7,500 important because it is the precise point at which landlords are imposing an equivalent loss on tenants. (Recall that Project A has a net present value of $1 million, and Project B has a net present value of $250,000. Project A is worth $750,000 more than Project B. At a relocation fee of $7,500 per tenant, the total cost imposed on tenants is $750,000.) Under simple fairness, $7,500 is the bright line by which respondents distinguish between fair and unfair behavior. What these results show is that in this scenario, the majority of respondents went beyond simple fairness and embraced complex fairness. That is to say, the majority of respondents answered this question in a way consistent with the proposition that one person should not achieve a relatively large gain by imposing a relatively small loss on another. In fact, we can be even more precise and restate our findings as follows: among those respondents who considered fairness as a constraint, they answered in a way consistent with the proposition that one person should not achieve a *$10* gain by imposing a *$7* loss on another ($5,316 divided by $7500 is approximately 70 percent).

Before closing this section, we must emphasize that the fact that this case is from the real estate industry is not irrelevant. We do not expect complex fairness to hold in every situation where simple fairness holds. In fact, the suggestion here has been that the community will demand complex fairness only where one party to the transaction is perceived as superior to the other party in some relevant characteristic. To begin to test this, we asked student respondents (as part of a follow-up questionnaire) whether or not they agreed with the following statement: "The real estate industry is unique. There is rarely a level playing field for landlords and tenants." A majority of respondents were more likely to agree with this statement than disagree (statistically significant difference). Not surprisingly, among those respondents who chose Project B in Case 2, this finding was even more dramatic. These results underscore the intuition that complex fairness is not a universal phenomenon. In situations where there is little difference between transactors (where there is a level playing field), it is doubtful that complex fairness will hold.

ENFORCEMENT

If both simple fairness and complex fairness exist as community norms, one wonders how such norms might be enforced, especially in those organizations where the rhetoric of profit maximization is also freely embraced. We can make a distinction between two sources of enforcement: external and internal constraints.

External constraints consist of the possibility of some kind of retaliatory action on the part of the injured party or parties. For example, tenants may set up a tenants' association and launch a rent strike, threaten a lawsuit, or plant negative stories about the landlord in the various media. To the extent that reputation and trust are important, intangible assets to the landlord, such retaliatory action can be a major expense in the long run. Importantly, KKT note that some transactors may even avoid exchanges with offending firms at some positive cost to themselves.

In addition to external constraints, internal constraints may exist. The existence of internal constraints suggests that landlords (and other transactors) may actually have a preference for simple and complex fairness rules. By introducing the notion of internal constraints, we are purposely opening up the intriguing possibility that some businesses may actually forgo relatively large profits even in the absence of expected, future long-run costs.

Given the existence of norms of fairness—both simple and complex—rational managers, as a practical matter, must determine the nature of these constraints. Do managers treat norms of fairness as external constraints imposed on the corporation by powerful stakeholder groups? Or, alternatively, are norms of fairness embedded in the internal structure of the organization? These questions are not asked and answered once and for all, but, rather, these questions are dealt with on an almost continuous basis. Each issue, whether environmental concerns, employee relations, or community responsibilities, requires managers to raise and grapple with these questions anew. For example, one can easily imagine an alternative energy company concluding that environmental responsibilities need to be pursued as part of a core strategy and are therefore considered internal constraints, whereas responsibilities to local communities are only peripheral to the company's identity and are regarded as externally imposed constraints. A local bank, however, with strong communal ties, might argue in exactly the opposite direction. For a local bank, communal responsibilities may be viewed as core concerns, but environmental issues may be treated as external in nature. Regardless of how managers finally answer these questions, the conversations and debates encouraged by openly posing and discussing these questions constitute a basic element of what it means to be an ethical organization.

FAIRNESS AS AN EXTERNAL CONSTRAINT

To the extent that fairness constraints are conceived of as external in origin, managers have adopted the commodity-based perspective, discussed in the previous chapters. Practical-minded managers who ignore fairness constraints are quickly reminded by forceful constituencies that rules have been broken. Here, the business ethics questions are essentially about power. Who really makes the rules? What do the rules require from business? What is the least costly way to comply?

To the extent that fairness is correctly conceived of as an external constraint, one of the major structural "solutions" to this kind of business ethics problem is the creation and maintenance of high-profile and powerful boundary spanners. Boundary spanners, according to Donna Wood, are

the people who gather information from and conduct transactions with stakeholders in the environment. Like the double-faced Roman god Janus, boundary spanners look both ways—inside and out—serving as gatekeepers for information and interpretations. They watch for signs of change, conflict, emerging needs and incongruities, and filter such information to people in the firm. They identify and respond to emergent threats and barely visible opportunities. (1996, p. 196)

Sensitive boundary spanners predict changes in public opinion before it is too late for corporations to take defensive actions. Powerful boundary spanners are able to convince top management to alter existing business relationships to conform to stakeholder demands, but only when those stakeholder demands will be enforceable.

Among boundary spanners, public affairs managers are perhaps most intimately associated with assessing the existence of externally imposed standards of fairness. According to the Public Affairs Research Group of Boston University (Post et al., 1981) the essential role of Public Affairs units appears to be that of a window out of the corporation through which management can perceive, monitor, and understand external change, and simultaneously, a window in through which society can influence corporate policy and practice. The boundary spanning role primarily involves the flow of information to and from the organization. (As quoted in Wood, 1996, p. 201)

In 1965, the Ford Motor Company provided a revealing glimpse into why companies establish public affairs offices. According to the company,

the officers and directors of Ford Motor Company firmly believe, and vigorously implement their belief, that governmental relations is a proper and necessary management function. They believe management has a responsibility to the stockholders to advocate the company's business interests vigorously and effectively before quasi-judicial hearings, legislatures, and administrative bodies. (Reid, 1965, p. 63)

While recognizing the differences in emphasis between the preceding two descriptions, it is readily seen that the language employed by both the Boston University Research Group and the Ford Motor Company to describe and justify the creation of a public affairs office is taken directly from the commodity-based perspective. Public affairs directors help top executives determine how to divide up the corporate pie when stakeholders disagree. Here, corporate social responsibilities are thought of as power constraints. This view is especially helpful when community norms are in the process of changing, and no consensus has emerged yet.

Consider, for example, the 1990 decision of the three major tuna producers in the United States to refrain from purchasing tuna caught with methods that trap and kill dolphins unnecessarily and to label their product as "dolphin-safe." The companies took these steps as a direct result of decades of protests by consumers and environmentalists. Undoubtedly, the tuna producers changed their corporate policies in spite of the fact that they were well aware that such new restrictions would be costly and would put them at a competitive disadvantage to other companies that did not adopt the new policies. This is not to suggest that managers, at the time the decision was made, believed that the change in policy would lower long-term profitability. Rather, the point is just the opposite. Managers undoubtedly factored in all the costs and all the benefits of the new policy and determined that, *on net*, producing "dolphin-safe" tuna was the profit-maximizing choice. In this case, it would seem that socially responsive managers viewed the newly emerging community norms as external in nature. The central idea here is that whether or not one agrees with the norms, from a practical perspective, one has to confront them head-on.

Donna Wood, in summing up her introduction to this topic, unabashedly advises that "the first step toward improving corporate social performance is for managers to recognize that performance expectations come *primarily from external stakeholders* and that social and political issues have tremendous impact on what is expected of companies" (Wood, p. 217; emphasis added). While wholeheartedly agreeing with the latter observation, I take strong issue with the first part of the pronouncement. Managers have to determine for themselves whether or not social performance derives from external or internal constraints. In those cases when it is merely an external constraint, then so be it. The commodity-based perspective is appropriate and efficient. But beware of treating true internal constraints as external.

A *Wall Street Journal* cover story about Chrysler's legal problems relating to the lift-up doors on its popular minivan illustrates the point. In October 1997 a federal jury awarded the parents of six-year-old Sergio Jimenez II, who was killed in a van crash, $262.5 million in damages, including $250 million intended to punish the Chrysler Corporation. The jury's decision reflected the belief that "Chrysler's negligent design and testing of the latch" had caused Sergio Jimenez's death (*Wall Street Journal*, November 19, 1997). At the time of this writing, Chrysler intends to appeal the verdict.

According to the *Wall Street Journal* account, a number of crucial factors led to the jury's decision:

- Chrysler marketed the van as a family vehicle, emphasizing safety features in advertisements, but used a latch variation abandoned by the rest of the industry in the 1960s. The company did alter the latches in 1988, but failed to inform owners of models already purchased.

- Chrysler allegedly destroyed films of mini-van crash tests, design documents, and other records.

- Allegedly, the latches could have been further improved for as little as 25 cents per car in 1990. Chrysler may have been afraid such a move would have undercut the assertion that there was no problem with the latches.

- In response to the expressed concerns of government regulators in 1994, Chrysler apparently attempted to exert political pressure rather than fix the problem. In a letter shown to the jury, Vice Chairman Tom Denomme wrote to Chairman Robert Eaton and President Robert Lutz, "If we want to use political pressure to try to squash a recall letter we need to go now."
- According to the *Wall Street Journal*, "Chrysler's Washington office mobilized, contacting the House Commerce Committee, which oversees NHTSA (National Highway Traffic Safety Administration) and where auto makers have an ally in Michigan's Rep. John Dingell, the committee's ranking Democrat . . . Chrysler helped committee staffers draft a letter criticizing the recall policy. It was signed by Mr. Dingell and Committee Chairman Michael G. Oxley and sent in January to Richard Martinez, NHTSA's administrator at the time." (p. A10)

Each of the elements just listed suggests perhaps that Chrysler's failure results from its insistence that safety is an external constraint and not an internal one in the automobile industry. Chrysler's failure to inform owners of possible safety problems and its decisions to allegedly destroy data, refrain from making low-cost improvements, and engage in aggressive lobbying all display a kind of gamelike quality reminiscent of Albert Carr's (1968) famous description of business ethics:

We live in what is probably the most competitive of the world's civilized societies. Our customs encourage a high degree of aggression in the individual's striving for success. Business is our main area of competition, and it has been ritualized into a game of strategy. The basic rules of the game have been set by the government, which attempts to detect and punish business frauds. But as long as a company does not transgress the rules of the game set by law, it has the legal right to shape its strategy without reference to anything but profits. . . . A wise businessman will not seek advantage to the point where he generates dangerous hostility among employees, competitors, customers, government, or the public at large. But decisions in this area are, in the final test, decisions of strategy, not of ethics. (p. 73)

The facts in this case, at least as disclosed in the *Wall Street Journal* report, reveal a company looking for the lowest-cost solution to a clearly perceived community norm. Instead of taking the lead in safety, as public pronouncements were implying, Chrysler adopted a defensive posture. The irony here is that by insisting on the inappropriate use of the commodity-based perspective, Chrysler performed worse even when measured only in terms of the commodity-based perspective.

FAIRNESS AS AN INTERNAL CONSTRAINT

If fairness constraints are to be thought of as internal in origin, managers must necessarily resort to the meaning-based perspective. James C. Collins and Jerry I. Porras have embraced such a view in their popular book *Built to Last: Successful Habits of Visionary Companies* (1997). The authors promote the notion of core ideology:

Core ideology ... defines the enduring character of an organization—its self-identity that remains consistent through time and transcends product/market life cycles, technological break-throughs, management fads, and individual leaders. ... Leaders die, products become obsolete, markets change, new technologies emerge, management fads come and go; but core ideology in a great company endures as a source of guidance and inspiration. (p. 221)

Although Collins and Porras do not break new intellectual ground, their enthusiastic endorsement of core ideology provides a model of how managers can and do think about meaning. The significant contribution of Collins and Porras is their demonstration through numerous examples, including discussions of Nordstrom, Hewlett-Packard, Procter and Gamble, and Merck (among many others), that a meaning-based perspective is a practical alternative to the purely commodity-based approach. The authors add, "Think of core ideology as analogous to the principles of Judaism that held the Jewish people together for centuries without a homeland, even as they spread in the Diaspora. Or think of it as like the truths held to be 'self-evident' in the United States Declaration of Independence, or the enduring ideals and principles of the scientific community that bond scientists from every nationality together with the common purpose of advancing human knowledge" (pp. 221–222). One of the important points from my perspective is the authors' insistence that core ideology is internal and not external. As they explicitly put it, "It is not derived by looking to the external environment; you get it by looking inside" (p. 228). Here, boundary spanners and public affairs officers are of little or no value. To be sure, to the extent that some norms of fairness are not contained in core values, managers are safe to treat them as externally imposed. This is certainly one reading of the tuna controversy discussed earlier. In many cases, however, norms of fairness derive directly from deeply held core values. In these situations, the norms define the identity of the organization. Here, norms of fairness are best thought of as internal in origin.

Laura Nash's description of Johnson & Johnson's decision-making process in response to the 1982 Tylenol crisis provides an excellent example of the practicality of treating norms of fairness as internal constraints. As news broke that several people in the Chicago area had been poisoned after taking Tylenol capsules laced with cyanide, executives at Johnson & Johnson faced an excruciatingly difficult decision. "No one could identify the source of the poisoning: was it a disgruntled employee, a manufacturing mistake, or had someone contaminated the capsules outside the plant, either en route to or in the stores?" (Nash, 1990, p. 38).

Even though experts at the time believed that it was unlikely that other forms of the Tylenol product were contaminated, in order to prevent copycat poisonings, Johnson & Johnson executives decided to recall all Tylenol products. At the time, Tylenol represented $100 million in annual revenues. While some people maintain that there was nothing extraordinarily ethical about the company's response, Nash believes that this decision reflected deeply held and fundamental beliefs of the company.

As James Burke announced at the outset, Tylenol tested the very core of assumptions driving the firm's past success. Johnson & Johnson had always maintained explicitly in its Credo and implicitly in its advertising that its primary concern was for its customers. Toward this end, J&J strongly emphasized product safety, quality and reliability. . . . But Tylenol was no longer reliable. Any strategy that hinted at a bias toward company profit over user interest or at the expense of public safety would deny these values. It would render the Credo claims dishonest and top management itself unreliable. In Burke's own words, their first priority was to remain true to the Credo. (Nash, 1990, pp. 39–40)

Does anyone really know why Johnson & Johnson decided to risk its $100 million cash cow by calling for a full recall of its product? Probably not. I am sure that there is some truth to those who claim executives framed this decision in the familiar terms of the commodity-based perspective. According to this view, norms of fairness were treated as externally imposed constraints. For these managers, the Tylenol crisis imposed significant constraints on profit-maximizing behavior, but the correct decision could be arrived at by upholding an unswerving commitment to long-run profits. On the other hand, Nash's alternative description undoubtedly also captures important aspects of the decision-making process. Internal constraints existed, as well. I don't know if, in this case, we will ever know which set of constraints was more important, but perhaps this is beside the point. The overriding message here is that a meaning-based perspective that openly promotes interpretation, discussion, and dialogue is already an important part of corporate culture among the very best organizations. Ethical interpretation is not something that happens only on lazy August afternoons by the water cooler. In the heat of battle, at the very moment of truth, ethical interpretation—what does an organization such as this do in a situation like this?—can define an organization for decades, if not longer.

One of the most significant lessons to be learned from the Johnson & Johnson case is the realization that a meaning-based perspective is of importance not only to individuals within the organization but to organizations themselves, which can be carefully designed to exploit such a perspective.

To be sure, a meaning-based perspective requires the backing of top management. Without strong leadership support, a meaning-based perspective is probably not possible. Without James Burke's undeviating engagement, Johnson & Johnson's Tylenol decision could not have been made in the way that it was. Significant individuals within the organization, no matter what the size of the organization, can make a difference. The point here, however, is that leadership alone is not sufficient.

In the case of Johnson & Johnson, the existence of the corporate credo was crucial (see credo below). Nash explains the decision-making process: "Thinking about profit would not suffice as a substitute for thinking about Credo commitments in noneconomic terms such as trust, health, safety, and public satisfaction" (p. 40). One manager told Nash, "Tylenol was the tangible proof of what top management had said at the Credo challenge meetings. You came away saying, 'My God! You're right. We really do believe this. It's for real. And we did what was right' "(p. 40).

The Johnson & Johnson Credo

We believe our first responsibility is to the doctors, nurses and patients, to mothers and fathers and all others who use our products and services. In meeting their needs everything we do must be of high quality. We must constantly strive to reduce our costs in order to maintain reasonable prices. Customers' orders must be serviced promptly and accurately. Our suppliers and distributors must have an opportunity to make a fair profit.

We are responsible to our employees, the men and women who work with us throughout the world. We must respect their dignity and recognize their merit. They must have a sense of security in their jobs. Compensation must be fair and adequate, and working conditions clean, orderly, and safe. We must be mindful of ways to help our employees fulfill their family responsibilities. Employees must feel free to make suggestions and complaints. There must be equal opportunity for employment, development and advancement for those qualified. We must provide competent management, and their actions must be just and ethical.

We are responsible to the communities in which we live and work and to the world community as well. We must be good citizens—support good works and charities and bear our fair share of taxes. We must encourage civic improvements and better health and education. We must maintain in good order the property we are privileged to use, protecting the environment and natural resources.

Our final responsibility is to our stockholders. Business must make a sound profit. We must experiment with new ideas. Research must be carried on, innovative programs developed and mistakes paid for. New equipment must be purchased, new facilities provided and new products launched. Reserves must be created to provide for adverse times. When we operate according to these principles, the stockholders should realize a fair return.

Obviously, it is not merely the existence of the credo alone, that made a difference here. More importantly, the corporate culture at Johnson & Johnson was such that reference to the credo not only was acceptable but was perhaps seen as necessary by top decision makers. Pertinent to this discussion is Edgar Schein's definition of corporate culture (1985):

[a] pattern of basic assumptions—invented, discovered, or developed by a given group as it learns to cope with its problems of external adaptation and internal integration—that has worked well enough to be considered valid and, therefore, to be taught to new members as the correct way to perceive, think and feel in relation to those problems. (p. 494)

At Johnson & Johnson, one of the "basic assumptions" developed by the group was that in order for the company to continue being itself, the company had to consider the safety of its customers as the primary factor in the decision-making process.

PRACTICAL IMPLICATIONS

Although the discussion in this chapter has been mainly theoretical, a number of important, practical implications emerge. We conclude this part of the discussion with some practical implications of the findings relevant to the real estate industry and beyond:

• Whether or not community norms of fairness are viewed as external or internal constraints, those who ignore them do so at their own peril. At minimum, managers need to ask themselves, Do we assign any weight to external costs imposed on noncontracting third parties, and if so, how much? Among other things, in the real estate industry, this implies that managers will have to attempt to estimate tenants' relocation fees, an admittedly difficult job.

- To economists, sunk costs are irrelevant. To the rest of us, sunk costs matter. In the case at hand, the initial cost of $1 million to buy the complex is probably a relevant fact, even though it is correctly categorized as a sunk cost. Given that we know fairness constraints depend on whether or not a firm is profitable (see discussion earlier), the larger this number (and therefore the smaller the expected profits are to the real estate company), the less likely that the community would expect one to forgo profits.

- Real estate firms, under pressure to forgo relatively large profits, may consider paying relocation fees for tenants and overlooking past rents that have not been paid. In fact, this is fairly common practice in the real estate industry.

- All things being equal, larger and better-known firms will need to pay more attention to fairness constraints. As a firm's reputation grows, managers will need to expend more resources protecting it. Growing real estate firms should not be caught off-guard by community standards that were not vigorously enforced when the firm began operations but are now more carefully scrutinized by the media and other stakeholders.

- Firms might consider treating different types of tenants in different ways. For example, those tenants with especially high relocation costs may be given preferential treatment. Local laws protecting handicapped or elderly tenants may not go far enough. Long-term residents with a history of paying their rent on time may be given special consideration when applying income-qualification rules.

- Those firms that believe they are meeting community standards of fairness may have to actively justify and explain their actions to other stakeholders. Such public relations efforts not only need to be sensitive to legal requirements but must honestly confront community norms of fairness.

This chapter has extended KKT's notion of simple fairness by trying to grapple with the question, How fair is fair? Community standards not only demand that one person should not achieve a gain by simply imposing an *equivalent* loss on another party, but, even further, community standards may demand that one person should not achieve a relatively large gain by imposing a relatively small loss on another party. We label this complex fairness. This chapter has demonstrated the existence of complex fairness in the real estate industry. Although we do not expect complex fairness to hold in every case where simple fairness holds, we do not think that there is anything special about the real estate industry except that the community perceives that landlords have an advantage over tenants.

NOTE

1. The basic question of this chapter is to determine whether or not complex fairness exists as a community norm in the real estate industry. To test this proposition cleanly, we want to study to what extent those students who are profit maximizers in the absence of external costs (Case 1) will begin to factor in costs imposed on third parties (Case 2).

5

Do Corporate Outputs Satisfy Human Needs?

Perhaps the title question of this chapter is the single most important one about business ethics. To the extent that corporate outputs satisfy or even partially satisfy human needs, there is a prima facie case to be made that these organizations meet minimal business ethics requirements. On the other hand, if corporate outputs fail to satisfy or, worse yet, stifle the satisfaction of human needs, how can business managers legitimate such outputs? Consider for a moment the case of cigarettes: does this product satisfy a real human need? (Pava and Krausz, 1997).

At first glance the title question seems disarmingly simple. Nevertheless, as we pause to consider it more carefully, the question of how to define human needs looms large. Do human needs really exist? If so, what kinds of desires should be included in this category? Finally, can organizations (including business corporations) help to satisfy human needs, even the highest-level needs? While recognizing that answers to these specific questions will be controversial, the questions remain important. In fact, this chapter suggests that how one approaches the subject of human needs, in large part, determines one's attitude toward business ethics.

MASLOW'S THEORY OF HUMAN MOTIVATION

More than 50 years ago, Abraham Maslow published a pathfinding study called *"A Theory of Human Motivation"* (1943). This work and follow-up studies by Maslow (1954, 1968) are still among the most systematic and thought-provoking approaches to the question of human motivation. In the 1943 paper, Maslow carefully described a hierarchy of human needs. According to Maslow's framework, after human beings satisfy (or partially satisfy) lower-level needs, higher-level needs begin to appear and to motivate new behaviors. In turn, when these new behaviors satisfy the recently emergent needs, Maslow suggested that yet another level of needs arises. In all, Maslow identified five levels of human needs that he believed were shared by most people regardless of cultural and other background factors. Among these "basic needs," as Maslow labeled them, are the (1) physiological, (2) safety, (3) love, (4) esteem, and (5) self-actualization needs. Each of these needs is now briefly defined and discussed.

Physiological Needs

Although Maslow made no formal attempt to identify specifically the physiological needs, he surely includes hunger, sex, and thirst here. Maslow makes the point that for someone who is lacking everything in life, the major motivating force is certainly the attempt to satisfy physiological needs. For example, he observed, the starving man thinks of nothing other than food. Once these lowest-level needs are met, however, higher-level needs immediately begin to emerge.

Safety Needs

Just as the hungry man thinks of nothing other than food, to someone who is in danger, nothing matters except safety. Interestingly, Maslow explicitly noted that most healthy adults in the United States are largely satisfied in their safety needs, but even in this culture we can still see the expression of safety needs in such areas as the "preference for a job with tenure and protection, the desire for a savings account, and insurance of various kinds" (p. 163). Among other things, this quote demonstrates that when Maslow uses the term "safety," he clearly has more in mind than mere "physical" safety.

Love Needs

If both the physiological and safety needs are satisfied, the love needs emerge. At this level, the individual "will feel keenly, as never before, the absence of friends. . . . He will hunger for affectionate relations with people in general, namely, for a place in his group, and he will strive with great intensity to achieve this goal" (p. 164). The need for human companionship begins to dominate this person's world. Maslow felt that the thwarting of these needs was the source for the most commonly found cases of "maladjustment."

Esteem Needs

Loved by at least some of the members of the group, the individual begins to think about his or her relative place in the group. The question of where one stands begins to take center stage. It is no longer sufficient to simply be an "average" member of the group; now one wants to achieve a certain degree of importance to the group. Maslow called these the esteem needs. Everyone, with few exceptions, has the need for both self-esteem and the esteem of others. Accordingly, Maslow divided esteem needs into two categories. "First, the desire for strength, for achievement, for adequacy, for confidence in the face of the world, and for independence and freedom. Secondly, we have what we may call the desire for reputation or prestige" (p. 165). The satisfaction of these needs leads to a feeling of importance, while the thwarting of these needs produces feelings of weakness and can eventually lead to severe neurosis.

Self-Actualization Needs

Even for the individual who has fully satisfied these four lower-level needs, for the individual who is both loved and respected by his friends and himself, a new and different kind of need develops, a uniquely human need. Maslow, following Kurt Goldstein, called this the need for self-actualization. "It refers to the desire for self-fulfillment, namely, to the tendency for him to become actualized in what he is potentially. This tendency might be phrased as the desire to become more and more what one is, to become everything that one is capable of becoming" (p. 165). It is almost as if after one is fully socialized as part of the group (and *only* after one is fully socialized), one has to step back and reinterpret oneself anew. This in no way, according to Maslow, implies that the self-actualized individual is a loner, aloof from the group. In fact, fully self-actualized individuals (having necessarily satisfied love and esteem needs) would have to identify strongly with their community.

Specifically, Maslow described some of the characteristics of the self-actualized person as follows:

1. Clearer, more efficient perception of reality.
2. More openness to experience.
3. Increased integration, wholeness, and unity of the person.
4. Increased spontaneity, expressiveness; full functioning; aliveness.
5. A real self; a firm identity; autonomy, uniqueness.
6. Increased objectivity, detachment, transcendence of self.
7. Recovery of creativeness.
8. Ability to fuse concreteness and abstractness.
9. Democratic character structure.
10. Ability to love. (1968, p. 157)

In an interesting explanation and extension to his discussion of self-actualization relevant to the subject of this book, the meaning-based organization, Maslow himself identified the cognitive desires to know and understand and explicitly linked these desires to the search for human meaning:

Even after we know, we are impelled to know more and more minutely and microscopically on the one hand, and on the other, more and more extensively in the direction of a world philosophy, religion, etc. The facts that we acquire, if they are isolated or atomistic, inevitably get theorized about, and either analyzed or organized or both. *This process has been phrased by some as the search for "meaning." We shall then postulate a desire to understand, to systematize, to organize, to analyze, to look for relations and meanings.* (1943, p. 166; emphasis added)

Maslow did not take his theory as self-evident; rather, he suggested it as an assumed hypothesis to be tested and validated empirically. He realized there could be exceptions to his hierarchy, the creative artist who goes hungry in the name of art, for example. He understood that a lower-level need might be only partially satisfied before the higher-level need kicks in. He recognized the fact that needs are often only partially understood by the actor, postulating that for most people needs are unconscious rather than conscious. He did not suggest that behavior is motivated by a single need but explicitly stated that human behavior has multiple motivations. To conclude this section, even with these caveats and limitations in mind, Maslow's writings represent an important and controversial statement about human motivation and needs. His theory provides a convenient and pivotal point of departure for anyone interested in examining the link between human needs and business ethics.

HUMAN NEEDS AND BUSINESS ETHICS

The thesis of this chapter is that one's theory of human needs, in large measure, is directly linked to one's theory of business ethics. In light of Maslow's framework, we can now be more specific about this thesis.

Rejectionists

First, there are those who assert outright, with seemingly no hesitation, that there are no such things as human needs, in fact, that the introduction of this construct represents a dangerous, misleading, and unscientific precedent. Let's label this view as "rejectionist." Its clearest and least equivocal articulation has been put forth by Jensen and Meckling (1994). To this group of thinkers, the assertion that there are no human needs inexorably leads to the conclusion that there is no such thing as business ethics. From such a perspective, asking whether or not corporate outputs satisfy human needs is pure nonsense or worse. Those who ask this question must have an ulterior motive.

Minimalists

A second position accepts the notion of human needs as a legitimate construct. In this sense, the minimalists clearly reject the rejectionists. This position, however, draws a distinction between lower-level needs and higher-level needs. To oversimplify, minimalists openly embrace the notion of physiological needs and safety needs. They may or may not accept the existence of love and esteem needs but surely reject as out of hand the idea of self-actualization as a basis for human motivation. The economist George Akerlof (1983) provides a clear and nuanced presentation of the minimalists' position. Unlike the rejectionists, minimalists potentially incorporate the notion of business ethics and view it as a legitimate tool of the business organization. It is suggested here, however, that while the minimalists' position is consistent with the commodity-based perspective of the business organization, it is inconsistent with the meaning-based perspective as discussed in earlier chapters.

Maximalists

Finally, a third group accepts and fully embraces the notion of human needs more or less as described by Maslow. This view interprets human needs in the widest possible way. Human beings are presumed not only to act to satisfy needs for food, sex, shelter, and safety but reasonably to attempt to satisfy higher-level needs as well, including, of course, the needs associated with self-actualization. This position is perhaps the most interesting in terms of linking it to a theory of business ethics. Can one embrace the notion of self-actualization and all that it entails and continue to insist, at the same time, that the business organization is merely a utilitarian tool to satisfy preconceived wants and preferences (as the commodity-based perspective insists)? Alternatively, if one adopts Maslow's theory in toto, is one then necessarily wedded to the meaning-based perspective of the organization? In other words, if human beings are, indeed, self-actualizers as Maslow suggested, must organizations necessarily be thought of as locations where human beings interpret life's meanings?

Maslow himself was the first to suggest an answer to these questions. "A society or a culture can be either growth-fostering or growth-inhibiting." While Maslow recognized that the sources of growth and human development are not created or invented by society, culture and structure can "help or hinder the development of humanness."

A gardener can help or hinder the growth of a rosebush, but cannot determine that it shall be an oak tree. This is true even though we know that a culture is a sine qua non for actualization of humanness itself, e.g., language, abstract thought, ability to love; but these exist as potentialities in human germ plasm prior to culture. (1968, p. 211)

Accordingly, it must follow that cultures and organizations within those cultures necessarily affect the likelihood that any given individual will or will not satisfy her or his need for self-actualization. The point is that if the need for self-actualization really exists (and is not merely a figment of Maslow's or our imaginations), it is impossible to design an organization that will (necessarily) have no affect on the individual member's ability to self-actualize. This is not to say that managers or even organizational theorists can easily predict or manage these effects or that they actually factor in these effects when making organizational design decisions. Simply put, like it or not, if the process of self-actualization occurs somewhere, it must occur everywhere, including the business corporation. A person's search for meaning is not a part-time vocation.

Among business theorists, Joseph L. Badaracco, Jr., discusses this issue most openly. Although he does not explicitly invoke Maslow's term, his view of human motivation is clearly consistent with the notion of self-actualization. Unabashedly borrowing from the writings of the controversial nineteenth-century philosopher Friedrich Nietzsche, Badaracco understands organizational man's primary goal as an attempt to satisfy Nietzsche's blunt, but powerful, dictum, "Become who you are" (Badaracco, 1997, p. 70). In the end, a careful reading of Badaracco's thought-provoking book *Defining Moments: When Managers Must Choose between Right and Right* suggests that his understanding of human motivation necessarily leads him to embrace a meaning-based perspective.

To summarize this discussion tersely, rejectionists reject not only human needs but also the possibility of business ethics. Minimalists embrace the commodity-based perspective of the organization but reject a meaning-based perspective. Maximalists fully embrace a meaning-based perspective.

THE PSEUDO-BUSINESS ETHICS OF THE REJECTIONISTS

Michael C. Jensen of Harvard University and William H. Meckling of the University of Rochester are heavyweights in the world of finance. Their frequently cited and studied paper on agency theory is a foundation of modern finance theory (1976).

I vividly remember presenting their findings to my teachers and fellow students in a doctoral seminar at New York University's Stern School of Business in the early 1980s. Appropriately, it was the very first paper assigned that semester, and it was my job to review it and explain it to the class. It was a heady and exciting time to be in business school, and Jensen and Meckling's agency theory, with its unapologetic endorsement of free markets and its insistence on self-interest as the one true model of decision making, symbolized our mood and aspirations (who ever thought about business ethics?) and set the tone and agenda for the remainder of the semester. The notes I made in the margins of the paper

(I still have the original copy in my files) remind me of the intellectual power and sway the authors once had on my thinking.

At the time I was not aware of (and it would have been out of place to mention, in any event, in a doctoral seminar on finance) the view of human motivation upon which their theory was built. As their more recent paper, "The Nature of Man" (1994), makes even clearer than does the original, Jensen and Meckling are out-and-out rejectionists. Putting it boldly, Jensen and Meckling insist that there are no such things as human needs. All talk of human needs is pure nonsense or worse. Explicitly indicting Maslow's notion of human needs and putting it in the strongest of terms, the authors now openly assert that the entire field of "behavioral science" has failed because of the "prevalence of Maslow's model" (p. 15).

Jensen and Meckling are nothing if not "pure" rationalists (Pava, 1997c). With no detectable irony whatsoever, Jensen and Meckling unveil a "set of characteristics that captures the essence of human nature, but no more" (p. 4). They label their model of human behavior REMM: the resourceful, evaluative, maximizing model. The process of discovering this model is described by the authors as follows: "REMM is the product of over 200 years of research and debate in economics, the other social sciences, and philosophy. As a result, REMM is now defined in very precise terms" (p. 5). Included among the so-called scientific discoveries is the following "postulate":

REMM is always willing to make trade-offs and substitutions. Each individual is always willing to give up some sufficiently small amount of any particular good (oranges, water, air, housing, honesty, or safety) for some sufficiently large quantity of other goods. Furthermore, valuation is relative in the sense that the value of a unit of any particular good decreases as the individual enjoys more of it relative to other goods. (p. 5)

The most important assumption of REMM for the present purposes is the following: "REMM implies that there is no such thing as a need. . . . There are only human wants, desires, or, in the economist's language, demands. If something is more costly, less will be wanted, desired, demanded than if it were cheaper" (p. 7). Admitting that this assumption arouses considerable opposition, the authors, nevertheless, contend that the failure to recognize this truth "is one of the most frequent mistakes in the analysis of human behavior" (p. 7). Referring to human needs—

or, one might add, responsibilities—is simply semantic trickery, a clever debating device, and no more.

George Bernard Shaw tells the story about the celebrated actress he meets on board a ship who first agrees to sleep with him for $1 million but then is indignant when Shaw counteroffers with a ten-dollar proposal. When the actress responds, "What do you think I am?" Shaw reportedly quips back, "We've already established that—now we're haggling over price." While Jensen and Meckling cite this story as the central evidence for the veracity of their theory, I think it's fair to point out that the only thing this story really proves is the existence of Shaw's imaginative sense of humor.

In any case, the point here is not to debate whether human needs exist or not; rather, the point is that if one accepts Jensen and Meckling's assumption about human needs, then one will also accept their implicit conclusion that there is no such thing as business ethics. To be fair to Jensen and Meckling, they never explicitly state this conclusion. In fact, the authors invoke the term "morality" in at least one instance: "Like it or not, individuals are willing to sacrifice a little of almost anything we care to name, even reputation or *morality*, for a sufficiently large quantity of other desired things (p. 7; emphasis added). But using the term "morality" in this way proves our thesis. A morality traded like a pair of used shoes at a flea market is no morality. Jensen and Meckling's use of the term "morality" clearly violates Norman Bowie's notion of business ethics as stipulated in the very first issue of the prestigious *Business Ethics Quarterly*, where he explicitly states that ethical actions often require one to act contrary to one's perceived self-interest (1991). Similarly, Edwin Hartman (1996) begins his book on business ethics by carefully noting up front that:

being moral is at least sometimes costly, especially in business: it can require self-restraint and occasionally self-sacrifice, and a clever but selfish person will have reasons to behave immorally. (p. 12)

Further along, he writes:

An essential purpose of moral behavior is to contribute to the ends, hence (ordinarily) the well-being, of people other than just the agent, *we should not consider moral any sort or system of behavior in which consideration of the interests of someone other than the agent plays no part*. The notion of that sort of morality makes no more sense than the notion of a pleasant sound that no hearers like to hear. (p. 16; emphasis added)

Business ethicists (including Bowie and Hartman, among others) would have a difficult, if not impossible, task defending managerial policies that attempted to manipulate employees' values and attitudes for the sole purpose of promoting managerial goals. Such a policy would violate Hartman's minimal definition of morality quoted before in that no consideration of the interests of someone other than the agent (in this case, the agent is the manager) plays a part in the strategy. Nevertheless, Jensen and Meckling conclude their paper (with apparently no degree of discomfort) by advocating that their theory provides the "foundation for thinking about how to change corporate culture" (p. 11) and thus ensure corporate success. Jensen and Meckling advise managers: "The values and attitudes of people within an organization will respond over time to view positively those actions which are rewarded in the organization and negatively those actions which are punished" (pp. 11–12). Telling managers to mold employees' values to promote one's own interest is a policy subject to criticism, but such criticism will stick only to the extent that it is assumed, to begin with, that employees have at least some legitimate human needs. In the absence of a theory of human needs, the business ethics enterprise cannot get off the ground. If all decisions, in the final analysis, are really only like the dilemma of whether or not one should have chocolate or vanilla ice cream for dessert tonight (i.e., simply a matter of tastes), it is difficult to conceive of what ethics, business or otherwise, might entail.

MINIMALISTS AND THE COMMODITY-BASED PERSPECTIVE

Life, for the most part, is dominated by the never-ending attempt to satisfy physiological and safety needs. We can never fully satisfy these needs, and so either higher-level needs never get a chance to emerge, or they simply don't exist. This description is the view of the minimalists, and it is clearly distinct from the views of both the rejectionists and the maximalists. Unlike the rejectionist position of Jensen and Meckling, minimalists, who distinguish between different kinds of needs, potentially incorporate the notion of business ethics and view it as a legitimate tool of the business organization. The thesis to be elaborated here, however, is that while the minimalists' position is consistent with the commodity-based perspective of the business organization, it is inconsistent with the meaning-based perspective. The preeminent economist George Akerlof best captures the spirit of the minimalist's position (1983). In Akerlof's world, it makes sense to think of human beings as choosing values solely for the purpose of promoting long-run material interests. In his words:

> Most persons attempt to choose values for their children (and perhaps also for themselves) according to their economic opportunities that allow them to get along economically . . . not only the wealthy . . . but also the poorest of the poor—immigrants, sharecroppers, and mountaineers—consciously teach their children values aimed at leading them best to survive economically. (p. 54)

Akerlof does not attempt to convince the reader of this core assumption of his model; rather, it is taken as self-evidently true. Our purpose is not to debate this point but merely to point out that such a position requires one to jettison the possibility that human beings might also pursue higher-level needs like Maslow's needs for love, esteem, and self-actualization.

To see this clearly, assume for the moment that Maslow is right. If these higher-level needs really exist, would not parents (contrary to Akerlof's assumption) choose values "that allow them to get along economically" but also choose values that would allow their children eventually to satisfy higher-level needs as well, where these needs are understood not only as tools to promote physiological and safety needs but as legitimate needs *in themselves*? In fact, if one accepts the need for self-actualization as legitimate and real (recalling Maslow's partial description of self-actualization as "the desire to become more and more what one is"), the whole notion of parents' choosing their children's values becomes deeply problematic. At minimum, somewhere in the theory, Akerlof would have to note that parents should choose values that will allow children to eventually interpret their own values and thus enhance the probability that their children might satisfy their need for self-actualization. All this, of course, assumes that Maslow is right. The easiest and best understanding of Akerlof, of course, is that higher-level needs simply don't exist. In other words, Akerlof is a minimalist.

This position, unlike Jensen and Meckling's, is consistent with a certain kind of business ethics, namely, the commodity-based perspective. Akerlof (1983) imagines a world where employers will pay honest employees more than they pay dishonest employees. Honest employees are not expected to embezzle, and therefore employers can afford to pay them a higher salary. In such a world, parents will choose to make their children honest if and only if the cost of doing so is sufficiently small. In such a way, parents ensure the economic well-being of their offspring.

According to the model here, it pays persons to bond themselves by acquiring traits that cause them to appear honest. And the cheapest way to acquire such traits according to our model is, in fact, to be honest! (p. 56)

In Akerlof's view, honesty and, more generally, ethics are real constructs with real functions. Consistent with the commodity-based perspective discussed earlier, ethics explains how the economic pie is carved up and is best thought of as a kind of power constraint. Further, individuals can act against their own narrowly perceived self-interest, as the following quote demonstrates:

In my model of childrearing, honesty may begin as a means for economic betterment, but then there is a displacement of goals so that the person so trained will refrain from embezzlement where there is no penalty. Psychological experiments with animals show similarly that animals may quite easily be trained to have dysfunctional behavior. (p. 57)

In this sense, Akerlof's view passes muster (perhaps just barely) with both Bowie and Hartman's minimal requirements examined earlier. Nevertheless, Akerlof's view is clearly inconsistent with the major assumptions of the meaning-based perspective. In Akerlof's world, where material satisfactions are the ultimate and only constant values in life, there can be little talk of organizations as locations where human beings interpret life's meanings. Akerlof's implicit suggestion that if parents could teach their children to feign honesty at a low cost, most parents would choose to do so is a direct contradiction of any vision of a meaning-based perspective.

MAXIMALISTS AND THE DISCOVERY OF THE MEANING-BASED ORGANIZATION

Consider the case of Steve Lewis, a bright, ambitious, energetic, twenty-something, African American financial analyst who has just completed his first year working at a prestigious New York investment bank. He is devoted and loyal both to his job and to his aspirations of moving up the ranks and someday making partner.

On a morning that started like any other, Lewis received a message asking him to participate in a presentation in two days to an important prospective client in St. Louis. Lewis was surprised by the invitation, as he knew little about the specialized area of municipal finance, the subject of the upcoming meeting, and because it violated company policy prohibiting analysts from attending client presentations.

After a preliminary investigation, Lewis discovered the reason for the somewhat unusual invitation. To put it in stark terms, the new state treasurer of Missouri, an important player in determining whether or not Lewis' bank would be selected, was black. As one of the partners, Andrew Webster, who was also African American, starkly explained to Lewis, "Listen, Steve, I hate for you to be introduced to this side of the business so soon. The state treasurer wants to see at least one black professional, or the firm has no chance of being named a manager for this deal. I'm used to these situations, but if you feel uncomfortable with it, maybe you don't have to go. I could try to change my schedule and go instead of you" (Badaracco, 1997, p. 10).

Lewis asked Webster for some time to consider his options and returned to his office, less naive, perhaps, than he had been just moments before. After pouring himself a cup of coffee, Lewis quickly understood his dilemma. He felt very strongly that business should hire, promote, and reward solely on the basis of talent and merit. He opposed playing games with race, gender, and religion. At the same time, however, he promptly observed that this was an incredible professional opportunity for him. After all, he had been selected over several senior people in the public finance group. This was an important and high-profile presentation. If his mere presence was all that was required to signal his loyalty and his dedication to the team, why not? The company, one way or the other, would surely make it worth his while. One might even suggest that this was a no-brainer. After all, nobody was asking the well-compensated Lewis to break any laws, and attending the meeting would surely promote his own interests, the interests of the bank, and even the interests of the client (at least, as the state treasurer seemingly defined those interests). On the face of it, it would seem to be a win-win-win situation: the company wins, the client wins, and Lewis wins.

At the moment of decision, Lewis noted to himself that his master of business administration (MBA) finance professor would have viewed this situation as simply one more opportunity to maximize profits and to satisfy individual preferences. His MBA finance professor, presumably well versed in Jensen and Meckling's agency theory, would have no vocabulary to help Lewis find his way through what he considered an ethical maze. In the absence of any notion of higher-level human needs, both rejectionists and minimalists offer little in the way of help. In this instance, what use is it to tell Lewis to promote aggressively his own interests or to choose those values that promote his own material welfare? These kinds of suggestions miss the essential point of Lewis' ill-defined, but keenly felt, dilemma. Lewis immediately recognized that whether he participated in the meeting or not, his choice would help to shape and define his developing character and personality. Lewis' problem, as he framed it, was not how best to get what he wanted but to come to know what is truly worth wanting. Lewis not only needed to identify his preferences and map out a clever strategy to satisfy those preferences but needed a way to judge and possibly alter his preferences. Although saying yes to the assignment would surely help Lewis and his firm, his attendance was "purely decorative: his role at the meeting was to serve as an African-American potted plant" (p. 67). Lewis wondered to himself whether participating in the meeting on such terms would make him a kind of house slave who enjoyed certain advantages and benefits unavailable to the field slaves in return for telling the master exactly what he wanted to hear. In other words, his own dignity and self-respect were on the line.

Understanding Lewis' dilemma and how he ultimately resolved it requires recourse to the language of self-actualization. As the case illustrates, it is unquestionably true that Steve Lewis was concerned about lower-level needs like safety, love, and esteem. But, as Badaracco (1997) points out in his perceptive analysis of this case, Steve Lewis' ultimate question is about who Steve Lewis is becoming:

Lewis faced a defining moment. His decision, whatever it was, would reveal something important about his character, values, and basic commitments in life. The situation would also test whatever values he had espoused in the past; he would now find out whether they were indeed his values or merely noble sentiments to which he had given lip service. Finally, his decisions and actions would shape his character, as well as his view of himself and the world—perhaps significantly. In essence, his choices would write a page of his moral autobiography. (p. 67)

Badaracco's fundamental insight (and what makes his book worth studying carefully and not just reading) is the assertion that when it comes to defining moments, life's primary task is to "become who you are." In order for Steve Lewis—and anyone else, for that matter—to negotiate complex ethical dilemmas (what Badaracco describes as right-versus-right conflicts), one needs to understand what one stands for. While this description of human motivation is attributed to the philosophy of Friedrich Nietzsche, the Prussian-born, nineteenth-century philosopher, it is also remarkably close to Maslow's notion of self-actualization described earlier. In the terminology introduced in this chapter, Badaracco is a full-fledged maximalist. If the thesis of this chapter is correct, then, one would expect Badaracco's theory of business ethics to move beyond the commodity-based view and to endorse a meaning-based perspective. His book provides a clean case study of the thesis we are exploring in this chapter.

To this point, it has been demonstrated that rejectionists (like Jensen and Meckling) reject not only the notion of human needs but any recognizable theory of business ethics as well. Minimalists (like Akerlof) believe that human beings are motivated only by lower-level needs. Either these lower-level needs can never be fully satisfied, or they are the only true human needs. Either way, self-actualization is an irrelevant and unnecessary theoretical construct, confusing the scientific deliberations rather than clarifying. Minimalists have a real, but thin, view of business ethics closely resembling the commodity-based perspective.

Maximalists accept, more or less, Maslow's theory of human motivation, including the possibility of self-actualization. What remains to be demonstrated is the link between self-actualization and the idea of the meaning-based organization.

THE MODEL OF APPROPRIATENESS TRUMPS THE RATIONAL MODEL

In Chapter 3, in answer to the question, How do ethical decisions happen?, it was argued that a key building block of the meaning-based organization is the kind of decision-making model in use. One of the main conclusions of the chapter suggested that individuals will have to learn to view decision making not only in terms of the rational model but also in terms of the model of appropriateness. If, indeed, Badaracco can be identified as a spokesperson for the meaning-based perspective, one would expect something like the model of appropriateness to play a significant role for his theory of business ethics. In fact, this is exactly what one finds!

One of Badaracco's most important practical conclusions is his advice that individuals faced with difficult ethical quandaries should learn to step outside themselves and pose the following four questions:

1. How do my feelings and instincts define the dilemma?

2. Which of the responsibilities and values in conflict have the deepest roots in my life and in communities I care about?

3. Looking to the future, what is *my* way?

4. How can expediency and shrewdness, along with imagination and boldness, move me toward the goals I care about most strongly? (1997, p. 82)

These questions are not identical to those identified in Chapter 3 as constituting the logic of appropriateness. In Chapter 3, the questions concerning recognition (what kind of a situation is this?), identity (what kind of a person am I?), and rules (what does a person such as I do in a situation such as this?) are formulated at a very high level of generality. Nevertheless, the point here is that if one answers Badaracco's more specific and nuanced questions, one is well on the way to answering the more general questions of Chapter 3. In other words, Badaracco's questions are consistent with the logic of appropriateness and are best thought of as a special case of, or one version of, the logic of appropriateness. Clearly, Badaracco's questions conflict sharply with the pure, rational model of decision making.

To see the connection between the two sets of questions, it's useful to compare them one by one. How does one answer March's first question concerning recognition? Its level of generality and purposeful vagueness beg for interpretation. One way of looking at Badaracco's first question, then, is that it provides a launching-off point. According to Badaracco, for one to "recognize" a situation, first one must turn inward and consult one's most primitive "feelings and instincts." One might conceive of other ways to recognize and define a situation (consult with clergy, invoke grand principles, examine corporate credos, etc.). Badaracco offers one solution among many other potential candidates.

I read Badaracco's second question as serving two distinct purposes. First, it offers additional guidance on the issue of recognition. Feelings and instincts are where one starts a process, not where one necessarily finishes. Feelings and instincts are thus viewed as necessary but hardly sufficient. One must also examine personal and communal history. In suggesting that decision makers must explore the "deepest roots" of responsibilities and values, Badaracco's second question is an attempt to "recognize" a situation in less subjective terms than his first question would allow. In other words, one asks oneself, Given my history and my culture, what is the appropriate way to distinguish among conflicting values? Badaracco's second question also helps one to begin to formulate an answer to March's second question, What kind of a person am I? Badaracco's second question asks one to flesh out the notion of identity. Badaracco's formulation strongly suggests that recognizing one's own identity is often a difficult problem and requires a kind of self-interpretation. Badaracco's version of the model of appropriateness highlights ideas pregnant in March's version but not quite fully born. Interpreting one's identity demands a high level of self-consciousness and communal awareness. Ethical quandaries are often opportunities to examine one's own identity. Is there a story that one can tell that weaves together the seemingly disparate events and decisions of one's life? Is the story consistent with one's community's self-understanding? Which of my felt values have the deepest roots? The individual is likened to a difficult text and, like a good literary critic, has to select the best and most meaningful interpretation.

Deep-rooted values alone are still insufficient, at least, according to Badaracco. His third question continues to probe the identity issue. Where his second question is backward-looking, the third question is future-oriented: What is my way? It's not enough to know where one has been; one must also target where one is going. The past never vetoes the future. I view this third question as an opportunity to combine the subjectivity of the first question with the objectivity of the second question. Answering Badaracco's third question may not yet provide a definitive answer to March's third question (What does a person do in this situation?), but at least it presents one possible set of directions, among others.

Badaracco's last question, what I like to call Machiavelli's reality check, bears the least resemblance to March's model of appropriateness. In fact, one way to understand Badaracco's last question is that it represents an attempt (a useful one at that) to integrate March's rational model with his model of appropriateness, noting especially the last phrase of Badaracco's question.

Neither March nor Badaracco would endorse a "recipe"-type approach to solving ethical problems as a quick reading of both sets of questions might initially suggest. March's model of appropriateness provides a broad framework. It points out elements of the problem a decision maker is well advised to consider and allows one to move beyond a strictly self-interested view of the world. Badaracco provides a set of slightly more specific questions. As is usually the case, the price of specificity is additional controversy. Many traditional ethicists might be concerned with Badaracco's heavy emphasis and seeming endorsement of subjective feelings and personal predilections. This is clearly much less of a concern with March's questions. Nevertheless, if one can accept Badaracco's version, it's probably of more practical help.

In the end, Steve Lewis himself demonstrates the use of the model. After much soul-searching, Lewis acknowledged his mixed feelings about attending the meeting (question 1) and traced out the roots of his feelings, recalling childhood memories of racist incidents his family endured (question 2). Nevertheless, he decided, in fact, to go to St. Louis but only after management promised that he would have 24 hours to prepare for the meeting and that he would be given at least some type of formal role. As it turned out, Lewis delivered a competent, twelve-minute presentation and even responded to a minor technical question.

He believed he had defined the dilemma soundly, at least in terms of his experiences and values. And, on the whole, he resolved it without betraying his parents and himself by merely attending the meeting and serving a decorative function. At the same time, his career prospects may have been strengthened. He felt he had passed a minor test, a rite of passage at his firm, and demonstrated that he was willing to do what it took to get the job done. The white analysts and associates who were passed over probably did some grumbling, but Lewis suspected that, if they had been dealt his hand, they would have played their cards as he did. (Badaracco, 1997, p. 83)

Steve Lewis' story hardly represents the final stage on the quest toward self-actualization; perhaps this incident merely records his first adult steps to finding his own unique voice, or perhaps it is simply a minor footnote in his moral autobiography. For the purposes of this chapter the story's importance is in demonstrating the inextricable link between self-actualization and one's decision model. A commitment to self-actualization implies a commitment to a broader view of decision making than mere self-interest, a core belief among advocates of the meaning-based organization.

ORGANIZATIONS AS LOCATIONS WHERE HUMAN BEINGS INTERPRET LIFE

If one accepts Maslow's notion that the highest type of motivation for behavior is the need for self-actualization, as Badaracco certainly does, one is led to embrace another central theme of this book, which is the assertion that organizations are often best described as locations where human beings interpret the meaning of life.

Organizations provide the context for our search for human significance. Participating in the richness and depth of organizational life often teaches us that what we think, do, and say matters, not just in a pragmatic sense but from a moral perspective as well. The eminent philosopher Charles Taylor has put this point more formally. He writes:

It is futile and wrong-headed to try to define common or mutual understanding as a compound of individual states. Our having a common understanding about something is distinct from my understanding it, plus your understanding it, plus perhaps my knowing that you understand, and your knowing that I understand; nor does it help to add further levels, say that I know that you know that I understand. This kind of convoluted situation sometimes exists in the more delicate or strained human relations, or on the diplomatic level between states. But it is recognizably distinct from the case where we have something out between us and come to a common understanding. (Taylor, 1995, p. 138)

Taylor's point here is that the notion of an organizational interpretation makes sense, and it is something of distinct human value.

As Badaracco makes plain, however, self-actualization is hard work. It almost always involves interacting with coworkers, customers, and other stakeholders in very sophisticated and subtle ways. It is not the kind of work where one labors to obtain scarce material resources or conventional power, however. The quest for self-actualization often requires one to "strategically" convince other stakeholders of the truth of one's interpretation of events and decisions in the organization. Interpretations are contested. Winning the day on a matter of interpretation is hardly the work of the solitary artist, hiding out in a cabin in lonely woods with only a mechanical typewriter for a companion, attempting to write the great American novel. Perhaps, the scarcest and most important resource of all is the organization's interpretation of the meaning of significant events, decisions, and activities. Managerial expert Jeffrey Pfeffer has emphasized this point:

The basic argument of a cognitive approach to the analysis of administrative action is: 1) social and organizational realities are, in part, outcomes of processes of social construction; 2) organizations, among other social entities, can be viewed as systems of shared meanings, entities in which there exists a shared consensus concerning the social construction of reality; 3) one of the tasks of management and a critical administrative activity involves the construction and maintenance of systems of shared meanings, shared paradigms, and shared languages and cultures; 4) language, symbolism, and ritual are important elements in the process of developing shared systems of belief and meaning, and become the focus and object of much administrative work; 5) a given organizational system's meanings are in contact, competition, and conflict with alternative views and belief systems held by other groups and in other organizations; which implies that 6) one of the elements of competition and conflict among social organizations involves the conflict between paradigms, defined as systems of beliefs or points of view. (1981, p. 9)

Managing corporate interpretations, however, is not for the weak of heart and is not always cloaked with nuance, as Gillette's Patton-like executive, John Symons, once demonstrated. At a meeting in Boston in 1987, Symons wanted to make the point that Gillette's future depended on convincing important stakeholders that shavers should be thought of as "fine instruments" and not commodities to be discarded after one or two shaves.

He listened patiently while the man in charge of refillables got up and gave a three-hour presentation. Then the man in charge of disposables, Bill Flynn, rose and began to speak. In his hand, he held a bag of ten Good News disposable razors—those blue plastic things—for show-and-tell purposes. He had barely started when Symons took the bag of disposables from him, threw it on the floor, and crushed it beneath his heel. "That is what I think about disposables," he said in a low gravelly voice. "Your review is not required." (Surowiecki, 1998, p. 46)

Symons and Flynn were not battling about who gets what (although the final resolution would clearly have material consequences) but were debating about the meaning of Gillette as a business enterprise.

Badaracco's brutal portrayal of the idealistic, but impotent, midlevel manager who pledges allegiance to family values but does nothing concrete to implement his vision underscores the need for viewing organizations as locations where human beings interpret the meaning of life. Specifically, Badaracco convincingly demonstrates that those who neglect or forget about managing interpretation are doomed to play an insignificant role in the corporation.

Peter Adario, head of marketing at Sayer MicroWorld, found himself in the middle of an ugly war between two of his underlings, Lisa Walters—37, single, hard-driving, and an ambitious product manager (she reported directly to Adario)—and Kathryn McNeil—late 20s, single

mother, also hardworking but struggling to find a livable balance between personal and professional commitments (McNeil reported directly
to Walters). McNeil had full custody of her six-year-old and no child
support from her ex-husband. While she was working 60-hour weeks,
everyone else was working even longer hours. Walters felt that, given
the pressure-cooker environment of wholesale computer sales, McNeil
could not provide the time, focus, and energy required to get the job
done. She was a laggard, and as such Adario should fire her. Walters
sent two handwritten notes to Adario explaining her qualms, both of
them unanswered.

As Badaracco paints this picture, Peter Adario just never got it. He
deluded himself into thinking that he could resolve his employees' conflict by sitting them both down in a room together and forcing them to
hash it out and come to a mutually satisfying agreement. Adario day-
dreamed that McNeil would explain to Walters about her family obligations, and, in turn, Walters would communicate her strong belief that
fairness and the incredible competitive environment required McNeil to
agree to spend more time on the job. Peter Adario possessed a strong
commitment to family values, and he wanted to signal his belief that it
was not just a nice-sounding slogan but a workable idea with important
and pragmatic implications. Adario reasoned:

By letting Walters and McNeil work out a solution, he would avoid being heavy-
handed or manipulative—they would "own" their plan, thereby making it more
likely to succeed. By getting personally involved and helping McNeil, Adario
was showing that he cared about the people in his unit. And, in his mind, the
tactic of keeping everyone at the table until they had all agreed on a plan would
remind everyone of the urgency of the company's situation. (Badaracco, 1997, p.
87)

As it turned out, Adario never got to implement his plan. After re-
turning from a presentation at a trade show, he was abruptly notified
that McNeil had been terminated. Walters had been working behind the
scenes with one of the firm's vice presidents and convinced the vice
president that McNeil had not been carrying her fair share of the load.
McNeil had been told to leave the premises that day.

Adario's mistake, as Badaracco perceptively explains it, was that he
failed to recognize that he was in the midst of a "contest for interpretations" (1997, p. 88). If, indeed Adario wanted to promote family values,

he had to fight for them and not just helplessly dream about them. Bad-aracco sums up:

Adario would have fared better if he had thought carefully about four important questions: What are the other strong, persuasive, competing interpretations of the situation or problem that I hope to use as a defining moment for my organization? What is the cash value of this situation and of my ideas for the people whose support I need? Have I orchestrated a process that can make the values I care about become the truth for my organization? Am I playing to win? (1997, p. 100)

If advocates of business ethics draw criticism, one version that often sticks is that business ethics is a kind of prison that prevents managers from doing what they really want to do (and what they really have to do to be good managers). In this view business ethics creates wimpy, passive managers who might complain a lot but can't do much to change economic realities. Badaracco reminds us that this need not be the case. In criticizing the overly passive Peter Adario, Badaracco demonstrates that the meaning-based perspective should be understood as business ethics in the active mode. If Adario really believed in family values, he needed to develop a program of action to implement them. He needed to convince others that his interpretation of reality was worth the time and effort that would be required to actualize it. I don't often agree with Milton Friedman. One thing he is right about, however, is that there are no "free lunches." Indeed, self-actualization in the context of the modern business organization is hard work.

FAIRNESS FROM THE INSIDE OUT

Yet another distinguishing characteristic of the meaning-based organization is the possibility that fairness constraints may be viewed as internal in origin, rather than as external obligations forced onto a reluctant business entity. Badaracco's forceful and unqualified endorsement of self-actualization as a primary motivator of behavior leads him here, as well.

If human behavior were solely motivated by the lowest-level needs, fairness as an internal constraint would make little or no sense. An individual or an organization that existed only to pursue material benefits would hardly be willing to entertain any thoughts of internal constraints. To the rejectionists and minimalists, the notion of an internal fairness constraint would be about as meaningful as music is to a deaf man. The existence of internal constraints would be viewed only as a nuisance, another obstacle to be avoided on the path to life's true rewards, material and physical comforts.

If, on the other hand, human beings have a need to express their unique talents and identities, to explore and find meaning in their lives, or in other words, if human beings do possess a need to self-actualize, then fairness constraints might play an integral role in the process. Many of us intuitively recognize that self-imposed constraints often serve as a well-earned signal to others that one has graduated into yet a higher stage of maturity and wisdom. An advertising agency that refuses to take on a lucrative tobacco account because management feels it's unfair to try to encourage more smoking (and not because the government says it's illegal) is, among other things, a better advertising agency. Only when advertising agencies have some theory that distinguishes between legitimate and illegitimate clients can they aspire to become meaning-based organizations. At the very best advertising agencies such a theory reflects internal considerations and debate as much as external constraints. Similarly, a textile mill that refuses to lay off all of its idle workers after a major fire and continues to pay them while it rebuilds its factories because it's the "right thing to do," as Malden Mills recently did, is an organization that not only is designed with survival in mind but strives to recognize the uniquely human ability to self-consciously evolve. In fact, the mere knowledge and awareness that one willingly abides by fairness constraints just as others abide by fairness constraints serve as a powerful motivating force to still more potential self-actualizers.

In Badaracco's most debatable case, he describes Edouard Sakiz's painful deliberations concerning the marketing of RU 486, the so-called abortion pill. In his role as chairman of the French drug company, Roussel-Uclaf, it was Sakiz's duty either to develop a marketing strategy for the extremely controversial drug (it had already been proven to be more than 90 percent effective in causing miscarriages if taken during the first five weeks of pregnancy) or to abandon the investment altogether. In Badaracco's portrait, Sakiz, unlike Peter Adario, knew what he wanted and went after it in single-minded fashion. Sakiz was a strong advocate for marketing the new drug.

One of the many interesting facets of this case revolves around the question of what was driving Sakiz's behavior and what led him to embrace a seemingly risky strategy for the company. Numerous powerful stakeholders were strongly opposed to marketing the new product. If RU 486 was ever to reach the market, Sakiz would have to play a sophisticated political game that would no doubt take up much of Sakiz's time and energy.

A diverse and powerful group of stakeholders opposed introducing the drug. First, numerous antiabortion groups were threatening an international boycott of the company if it decided to market the drug. Second, Hoechst, the German chemical company that owned a majority of Roussel-Uclaf's stock, was strongly opposed to marketing RU 486 and for seemingly good reasons. Its chairman was a deeply religious man and was opposed to abortion on moral grounds. He also felt that selling the drug violated both Hoechst's and Roussel-Uclaf's corporate credos. Hoechst's credo stated that its mission was to "meet people's basic needs and improve the quality of life while safeguarding and raising living standards." It was a particularly powerful document in the minds of many as it had been initially written in response to the company's role in the Holocaust; Hoechst had produced Zyklon B, which had been used by the Nazis to murder million of Jews during World War II. Roussel-Uclaf's credo unambiguously pledged the company to "placing our energy, our ideas, and our dedication in the service of Life." Third, Hoechst, other stockholders, and even Sakiz himself did not believe that profits alone could justify a decision to market the drug. Revenues from the sale of RU 486 were not expected to be especially high, profits would be harmed by the fact that the company was planning on selling much of the product to Third World countries at cost, and other product lines could be harmed by the threatened boycott. Lastly, even employees and managers were deeply divided about what to do. For example, the executive committee was split, with two members favoring the production and sale of the drug and two against.

With such a formidable list of opponents coupled with the questionable financial prospects deriving from RU 486, what was motivating Sakiz? Badaracco, not at all surprisingly, considering his unstinting endorsement of self-actualization, chooses to view this as a case of a manager's seizing the moment and recognizing an opportunity to clarify and define the fundamental values of the company and a vision describing the company's role in society, if not once and for all, at least for a good long while. In the terms of this book, Badaracco believes that Sakiz was trying to implement his view of fairness.

In the early part of his career, Sakiz, himself a medical doctor, had worked on developing the active chemical ingredient in RU 486. He thus had a deeply felt, personal stake in the final decision. "He believed strongly that the drug would help thousands of women, particularly in poor countries, avoid injury or death from botched abortions. In the developed world, he believed, RU 486 would provide a valuable alternative to surgical abortions" (Badaracco, 1997, p. 20). It was Sakiz's belief (at least as described by Badaracco) that these goals not only were consistent with his vision of Roussel-Uclaff as a pharmaceutical company but would help sharpen the vision among competing stakeholders. In other words, according to Badaracco, fairness, not as defined by the numerous stakeholders exerting external pressure on the firm, but fairness as internally construed, drove this decision.

Although, in the final analysis, I strongly disagree with the ethics of this case, it is important because it unquestionably demonstrates the live option of fairness as an internal constraint. Sakiz finally got his way by forcing a vote of the executive committee. Ironically, he voted against introducing the drug and favored suspending distribution. This seemingly counterintuitive move forced Sakiz's allies, especially the French government, to step in. As it turned out, the French government threatened to transfer the patent to another company that would market the drug. Roussel-Uclaf was thus able to reverse itself and market the drug, but now under the seeming protection of the government. Sakiz obtained his ultimate goal and avoided the pitfall of publicly proclaiming his real intentions. Badaracco justifies such seeming hypocrisy by stating that public leaders must follow a "special ethical code, one that differs from their private morality and from Judeo-Christian ethics" (p. 108). Badaracco elaborates that "only a naive manager would think otherwise" (p. 109). Such pronouncements are justified by a quote from Isaiah Berlin:

To be a physician is to be a professional, ready to burn, to cauterise, to amputate; if that is what the disease requires then to stop half-way because of personal qualms, or some rule unrelated to our art and its technique, is a sign of muddle and weakness, and will always give you the worst of both worlds. . . . *There is more than one world, and more than one set of virtues: confusion between them is disastrous.* (Berlin, 1980, p. 39; emphasis added)

Badaracco almost convinces me that there are situations where the ends justify the means. He comes much less closer to convincing me that there is more than one world and that Judeo-Christian ethics are naive; here, I'm still of the old-fashioned, one-world perspective (Badaracco himself at one time also accepted the one-world view—see, e.g., Badaracco and Ellsworth, 1989, p. 206). Nevertheless, what is not arguable is that his interpretations of this last case and the two proceeding ones provide strong evidence of the overriding thesis of this chapter, which is that there is a strong link between one's theory of human needs and one's theory of business ethics.

CONCLUSION

Stephen F. Goldstone, the chairman and chief executive officer of RJR Holdings Corporation, which owns R. J. Reynolds, the nation's second largest tobacco company, recently defended his industry as follows: "I have no moral view of this business . . . I viewed it as a legal business. You shouldn't be drawing a moral judgment about a business our country says is perfectly legal and is taxed like crazy by it" (as quoted by Jeffrey Goldberg, 1998, p. 41). If human needs don't exist, and everything is really a matter of taste, as the minimalists put forth, Goldstone's view is unassailable. Attacking Goldstone's defense of the industry would make about as much sense as attacking his taste in ties. But if Goldstone wants to convince the rest of us—who do believe in the existence of human needs—he would be well advised to search out, explore, and carefully communicate a moral foundation to serve as a defense for his livelihood and the thousands of others in the industry who depend upon him. A good place to start would be an answer to the following question, What legitimate human needs do cigarettes satisfy?

6

Is There a Role
for Religion in Business?

The meaning-based perspective suggests that religious and spiritual values will increasingly impact business decision making. For good or bad, the opportunities and problems associated with the mixing of religion and business will become ever more prevalent. Experts on corporate social responsibilities not only will have to consider how to ensure that religious men and women are not discriminated against in the workplace, a typical commodity-based issue, but will be called on to consider how the corporation can best accommodate and appropriate religious values. To some extent this is already happening, as many business practitioners and academics are turning to religious sources as a way of approaching and answering difficult questions related to business ethics not only at the level of the individual but at the level of the organization. There now exists a relatively large literature that attempts to integrate business decisions and religious values. The integration, however, is not without difficulties. For many, religious ethics provides the basis and the ultimate authority for a morally meaningful life. At the same time, in certain contexts, it is often assumed to be inappropriate to rely on, and to publicly justify decisions on the basis of, this ethics. Most importantly, is a religiously grounded business ethics consistent with the idea of political liberalism? While this question is fundamental and straightforward, to date it has received little, if any, careful attention.

ROBERT ALLEN, AT&T, AND WHO MAKES THE RULES?

AT&T's chief executive officer, Robert Allen, recently made the following ambivalent comment declaring his uneasiness over the corporation's decision to eliminate 40,000 jobs:

Increasing shareholder value is the right incentive for me to have at AT&T. Is it the right incentive for me to affect 40,000 people? Hell, I don't know. . . . Is it fair? Hell, I don't know if it's fair. I don't make the rules. (As quoted in *Newsweek*, January 15, 1996, p. 37)

In this brief quote, Allen concedes that the question of ethics is a difficult one but ultimately irrelevant to the business executive at a practical level. The inherited "rules" state that the maximization of shareholder value trumps "fairness" every time. This belief is under increasing examination. But, if Allen's statement (if not his decision) is wrong, as I think it is, how do we know?

Increasingly, many business practitioners and academics are turning to religious sources as a way of approaching and answering such difficult questions. There now exists a relatively large literature that attempts to integrate business decisions and religious values. The general conviction that man is created in the image of God and the overarching biblical command to love one's neighbor are viewed by religious men and women as deeply held, transcendent values that may be seen to conflict with an ethos of pure profit maximization.

This integration, however, is not without its own difficulties. In a pluralistic democracy such as the United States, aren't we all better off if we mutually agree to set aside personal, religious values when making public decisions, especially those decisions unilaterally affecting the lives of thousands of people who do not share our own religious convictions? A simple thought experiment underscores this point. Suppose that Robert Allen had decided that in spite of the enormous competitive disadvantages of forgoing the layoffs, his understanding of specific biblical passages required him, as a devout Christian, to keep all current employees. He is convinced, based both on his own reading of the Bible and on the authority of religious leaders, that the Bible is unequivocal on the impermissibility of suddenly terminating huge numbers of employees. He acts on the directives of his religious convictions and justifies his action, in the president's letter to shareholders and through other media, by invoking specific biblical verses. He does so in spite of the fact that he also believes and states that, in the long run, it is a losing strategy for shareholders. Surely, such a response on Allen's part would be at least as unpalatable as the response he actually gave. Critics would correctly point out that the hypothetical response puts too great an emphasis on personal, religious beliefs. Critics would certainly charge that it is unfair to promote one's own moral and religious agenda in the corporate arena. They would continue that a chief executive officer can allocate his own resources based on his own reading of the Bible, but it is out of bounds to invoke a religiously grounded ethics in this public context.

It would seem, then, that the situation is almost impossible. For many, religious ethics provides the basis and the ultimate authority for a morally meaningful life. Yet, at the same time, in certain contexts, it is often inappropriate to rely on, and to publicly justify action on the basis of, this ethics. With this difficulty in mind, the main goal of this chapter is to answer the following specific question. Is a religiously grounded business ethics consistent with the idea of political liberalism? While this question is fundamental and straightforward, to date it has received little, if any, careful attention.

The chapter rejects two plausible, but extreme, approaches to this question. The first approach assumes that business is purely "private." In this view, business decisions are best characterized as voluntary, contractual agreements among equals, with virtually no third-party effects. Given that political liberalism is a theory solely devoted to public matters or issues of state, the original question immediately dissolves. According to this view, it is not so much that religious business ethics is consistent with political liberalism but that business ethics deals with a completely different domain. Proponents of this view might not agree with Allen's hypothetical response but would not view his reliance on religious sources and authorities, per se, as problematic. A second approach, diametrically opposed to the first, begins with the assumption that business decisions, at least at the managerial and board levels, are purely "public." Business managers and board members possess huge power to affect the allocation of scarce resources within the national and international economies. These decisions necessarily impact on questions related to basic issues of justice. Corporations are public institutions, and managers are correctly compared to government officials. Under the additional and widely accepted assumption that government officials and other citizens should attempt to observe a strict and complete separation between religiously grounded ethics and their public decisions, it easily follows that corporate managers must do the same. Proponents of this view, especially those who accept a religious worldview, would reject outright any direct reliance on religious texts and authorities as a basis for corporate decisions but might still be deeply disturbed by Robert Allen's response.

Is a religiously grounded business ethics consistent with the idea of political liberalism? If business is purely private, the answer is surely yes. If business is purely public, and if political liberalism demands that government officials and other citizens observe a strict and complete separation between religion and state, the answer is just as surely no.

This chapter takes as its point of departure that neither of these two extreme views is adequate. First, corporations are neither purely private nor public but, rather, are best characterized as "quasi-public" institutions. This characterization, discussed later, implies that political liberalism may dictate that there exist situations in which invoking religious business ethics is inappropriate. The point is that once one removes the assumption of business as a purely private matter, the justification of a religiously grounded ethics in the context of a politically liberal democracy becomes problematic. On the other hand, such an assumption should not be taken to imply that all religiously grounded business ethics are always inappropriate. As this chapter demonstrates, it is far from obvious that even government officials need to observe a complete separation between religion and state in formulating, justifying, or expressing public policies, even policies leading to so-called coercive results. If so, it follows that managers of quasi-public institutions may, under appropriate and limited circumstances, invoke and rely upon a religious, albeit private, worldview. The remainder of this chapter explores the precise contours of these "appropriate and limited circumstances."

CORPORATIONS AS QUASI-PUBLIC INSTITUTIONS

It is widely acknowledged that the philosopher John Rawls has provided the most important theoretical description and defense of political liberalism (Rawls, 1971, 1993). Whether or not one fully endorses his detailed view, it is important to examine to what extent the philosophical idea of political liberalism is consistent with religiously grounded business ethics. Rawls views the fundamental political question as follows: "How is it possible for there to exist over time a just and stable society of free and equal citizens, who remain profoundly divided by reasonable religious, philosophical, and moral doctrines?" (1993, p. 4). A major feature of his answer, already pregnant in his original formulation of the question, is the insistence that a political conception of justice is best thought of as a "freestanding view" (1993, p. 10). By this he means, among other things, that a political conception of justice is fundamentally independent of all full-blown, comprehensive doctrines. Comprehensive doctrines, be they philosophically or religiously grounded, are wide-ranging conceptions that are universal in scope. Further, such a doctrine is a "precisely articulated system" (p. 13) that, in the limit, addresses all moral and ethical issues. Many such reasonable, comprehensive doctrines exist alongside one another in a pluralistic democracy. In sharp contrast, the theory of political liberalism self-consciously limits itself as "a moral conception worked out for a specific kind of subject, namely, for political, social, and economic institutions" (p. 11). Rawls believes that constitutional questions and questions of basic justice can be discussed and answered only by invoking public reasons and need not—and, in fact, cannot—rely on existing comprehensive doctrines. Public reasons "appeal only to presently accepted general beliefs and forms of reasoning found in common sense, and the methods and conclusions of science when these are not controversial" (p. 224). Although he does not state it in these terms, his theory suggests the commonsense view that political liberalism is possible to the extent that public institutions are ruled by public reasons only.

It is far from obvious, however, how advocates of political liberalism would classify the modern business corporation. While Rawls explicitly recognizes the legitimacy of churches, universities, "and other associations in civil society" (1993, p. 213) to utilize nonpublic reasons, he is silent with regard to business corporations. Stated more formally, in the theory of political liberalism, the boundary between the public and private spheres is not always well specified. For those interested in elaborating a viable business ethics from a religious perspective (or, for that matter, on the basis of any comprehensive doctrine), this limitation of the theory needs to be examined carefully.

Although Rawls does not provide specific discussion of the business corporation, he does draw a general sketch of the public domain. From this sketch, details can be extrapolated. Rawls emphasizes that the public/private distinction and hence the theory of political liberalism rest on the qualitatively different types of relationships that exist in each sphere.

The two key, distinguishing variables of the public domain relate to membership and power. We are members of a political society without regard to our own wishes. We are born and die within the confines of political society, whether we like it or not. Second, in the public sphere, we are all vulnerable to the legitimate use of coercive power, which, if it means anything at all, must imply that on occasion we will be forced to act, or we will be acted upon, in ways against our own immediately perceived self-interest.

From this brief description, it is clear that the corporation is not a purely public institution. No one "materializes" within the corporate setting, nor is it felt by members of the corporation to be impossible to exit. Further, the corporation, while often extremely powerful, can never resort to the use of "force" to obtain its goals. It would be a critical mistake, however, to conclude that because the business corporation fails to satisfy completely these criteria, it in no way resembles the public sphere. It is more useful to think of the public/private distinction in terms of a continuum.

Government institutions come the closest to satisfying Rawls' ideal criteria of the public sphere. But it should be noted that even with regard to the government, political society is never completely "closed." There are always laws controlling immigration and emigration, and there exist significant limits to the government's use of power. Rawls is certainly correct when he notes that "leaving one's country is a grave step" (1993, p. 222), but, it needs to be emphasized here, it is almost never an impossibility. The question of the status of the corporation within the theory of political liberalism should not be conceived of as either/or. Real-world institutions are never completely private or wholly public but are "more or less" public or "more or less" private. At this point, the loss in analytical rigor is worth the gain in descriptive accuracy.

It is readily acknowledged that business organizations share some of the characteristics associated with those institutions usually classified as private, such as synagogues, churches, or universities. For example, in a democracy characterized by political liberalism, worshipers are relatively free (for whatever reason they perceive as important) to leave their synagogue and join or form another or simply stay home. The use of force to prevent someone from attending a religious service, no matter how "unorthodox" the service, is impossible to justify from the perspective of political liberalism. Similarly, if employees, customers, or suppliers are unhappy with a particular corporate policy (they might believe the policy violates a deeply held moral or religious value), they can, at times, exit the relationship at relatively low cost. In turn, it would be illegitimate for a corporation to apply force or even the threat of force to coerce employees to carry out a corporate policy against their will. In this limited sense, private enterprise is close to being truly private.

More importantly, however, businesses, especially the huge, publicly traded corporations, often reveal characteristics usually associated with public institutions. In fact, David Ewing, former editor of the *Harvard Business Review*, notes that many corporations have larger "populations" than the original thirteen colonies (1977). The author specifically documents the following revealing statistical comparisons:

AT&T has more than 939,000 employees, nearly twice the size of the largest colony, Virginia, which had about 493,000 inhabitants in 1776.

General Motors, with 681,000 employees, is nearly two and one-half times the size of the second largest colony, Pennsylvania, which had a population of about 284,000 people in 1776.

Westinghouse, the thirteenth largest corporate employer today with 166,000 employees, is four times the size of the thirteenth largest colony, Delaware, which had a population of 41,400. Westinghouse's "population" is also larger than that in 1776 of South Carolina, New Jersey, New Hampshire, Rhode Island, and Georgia. (Ewing, 1977, p. 26)

These data lead Ewing to describe corporations as "minigovernments." I prefer the expression quasi-public.

Size alone, although important in its own right, is not a sufficient criterion. The key variables in the theory of political liberalism, as outlined earlier, are membership and power; and while it is sometimes the case that it is relatively easy to leave the corporation and extricate oneself from its effects, this is not always or even usually true. Ewing, for example, further portrays corporations as follows:

They pay salaries and costs. They have medical plans. They provide for retirement income. They offer recreational facilities. They maintain cafeterias. They may assist an employee with housing, educational loans, personal training, and vacation plans. They schedule numerous social functions. They have "laws," conduct codes, and other rules. Many have mechanisms for resolving disputes. A few even keep chaplains on the payroll or maintain facilities for religious worship. (p. 260)

Even traditional libertarians (Friedman, 1962, 1970; Friedman and Friedman, 1980) who endorse the position that the goal of the corporation is to maximize profits for the sole benefit of shareholders cannot maintain the fiction that corporations are purely private institutions. More often than not one is a "member," in a broad sense, of a corporation whether one likes it or not, and one is subject to corporate power, even if against one's will. To the extent that these characterizations hold, political liberalism would insist on treating the corporation like any other public institution.

Even libertarians recognize that corporate managers attempt to:

1. create and sustain monopolistic markets,

2. impose costs or externalities on noncontracting third parties, and

3. lobby governmental officials for the personal and corporate gain.

The point, here, is not to judge and condemn these activities. Clearly, some actions properly falling within these categories can easily be defended and justified in terms of economic efficiency, while others are a direct result of the current political and economic system. Rather, the point is to indicate how each of these activities demonstrates the quasi-public, as opposed to private, nature of the corporation. If the public/private distinction is a continuum, the existence of monopolies, externalities, and corporate lobbying tilts one's judgment of business toward the public pole.

CORPORATIONS AS CREATORS OF MONOPOLIES

Managers have a built-in incentive to try to reduce competition. Corporations attempt to discover and create consumer demand for their own products. Managers, usually with the help of government, can potentially create monopoly-like conditions and thus improve profitability and stability in many different and creative ways. In the pharmaceutical industry, for example, companies seek and obtain patents to protect the costly investments incurred in the process of researching and developing a drug. Often, the underlying technology is, at least in part, based on publicly funded research. Further, many industries require special licensing requirements. For example, accountants are required to pass the certified public accountants exam before they are allowed to audit corporate reports. While unquestionably, this requirement protects the public from some unscrupulous, would-be charlatans, the practice also provides accountants who are in charge of writing and administering the exam a high degree of control over membership in the profession. Automobile companies benefit from high tariffs and quotas on foreign imports. The economy as a whole may or may not benefit from this kind of protective legislation in the form of increased domestic employment, but, as with licensing requirements, huge power is amassed by the protected industries, in this case, the automobile manufacturers. Some corporations are the beneficiaries of special regulations that recognize the company as the sole producer of, say, electricity, telephone, or cable service in a particular area. As before, this practice may be justified from an economic perspective, but it almost automatically creates huge and powerful corporations that begin to look, in many ways, like public institutions. It remains true that a patient in need of a patented drug or an electric utility customer can always choose not to engage the corporation, but the degree of choice here resembles that of a citizen's choosing to emigrate from his or her home country more than choosing laundry detergent or toothpaste. Even if corporations begin their lives as private institutions, managers are almost always strategically engaged in a process of transforming them into publicly active entities.

CORPORATIONS AS CREATORS OF EXTERNALITIES

If the goal of the corporation is to maximize profits for the sole benefit of shareholders, as libertarians insist, it follows that managers will seek out ever more creative ways to impose costs on noncontracting third parties. They attempt to create externalities in order to benefit the corporation, which is equated with shareholders. Whether or not one agrees with this rather pessimistic and amoral view, the mere existence of externalities is noncontroversial.

The classic example is pollution. A person living downstream from a factory that dumps its waste products into the river bears part of the cost (in the form of fewer fish, unpleasant odors, loss of recreational facility, lower property values, moving costs, etc.) of the factory's products. Once again and even more so than in the case of monopolies, one is often a "member" of the corporation simply by being a neighbor, even if against one's will. The Exxon *Valdez* and Bhopal/Union Carbide disasters are extreme examples of what is at stake. They differ only in magnitude from the typical and everyday corporate externalities. In describing the responsibility for corporate impacts Peter Drucker (1989) amplifies:

It has to exercise considerable control over the people who work for it; otherwise, it cannot do its job. It has considerable impact on people who are customers whether they buy a company's goods or are patients in a hospital. And it has impacts on bystanders. The factory that closes at four-thirty in the afternoon creates a traffic jam for everyone in the community. Responsibility for one's impacts is the oldest principle of the law. It does not matter whether the institution is at fault or is negligent. The Roman lawyers who first formulated this principle called it the "doctrine of the wild animal." If the lion gets out of its cage, its keeper is responsible. Whether the lion's keeper was careless and left open the door of the cage, or whether an earthquake released the lock, is irrelevant. (pp. 87–88)

The producer of externalities (be they positive or negative) is nothing if not, at least, quasi-public.

CORPORATIONS AS LOBBYISTS

I can do more for General Electric by spending time in Washington and assisting in the development of responsible tax policy than I can by staying home and pricing refrigerators. (Reginald Jones, former CEO of General Electric on lobbying)

Corporations can be public in more direct ways. Even if corporations are not monopolists or do not benefit from the imposition of costs on bystanders, most major corporations are engaged in some form of political lobbying activities. It is believed that "business has a legitimate right to participate in a political process, just as consumers, labor unions, environmentalists, and others do" (Frederick, Post, and Davis, 1992). Managers and board members attempt to affect the outcome of elections and help pass corporate-friendly legislation. Weber (1996) recently described the process as follows:

Lobbyists are successful in affecting the political process because they are successful in becoming an important part of the process. They provide lawmakers with information that lawmakers cannot get easily otherwise; lobbyists contribute and raise money that legislators need for re-election; they assist staff in drafting or revising legislation; they accompany lawmakers at many social and speaking events; they become friends with legislators. (p. 255)

Lobbyists thus play an important role in the political process. On the positive side, corporations can often be a source of important and low-cost information to legislators.

Sometimes, however, the central role of corporate lobbyists leads critics to question the integrity of the process. In 1977, Mark Dowie wrote a scathing attack on Ford Motor Company's successful attempt to lobby government regulators for easier automobile safety standards. The author implies that Ford's lobbying effort eventually contributed to between 500 and 900 preventable burn deaths caused by engineering limitations in the Ford Pinto.

The particular regulation involved here was Federal Motor Vehicle Safety Standard 301. Ford picked portions of Standard 301 for strong opposition way back in 1968 when the Pinto was still in the blueprint stage. The intent of 301, and the 300 series that followed it, was to protect drivers and passengers after a crash occurs. Without question the worst post-crash hazard is fire. So Standard 301 originally proposed that all cars should be able to withstand a fixed barrier impact of 20 mph. . . .

When the standard was proposed, Ford engineers pulled their crash-test results. . . . But with the Pinto particularly, a 20 mph rear-end standard meant redesigning the entire rear end of the car . . . adoption of this standard would have created a minor financial disaster. So Standard 301 was targeted for delay, and with some assistance from industry associates, Ford succeeded beyond its wildest expectations: the standard was not adopted until the 1977 model year. (p. 29)

Hoffman (1995) and others have used this case to question the legitimacy of corporate lobbying. Are some forms of lobbying more benign or more necessary than others? Is the Pinto example typical or an exception to the rule? One need not take a position on these important and difficult questions for the present purposes. The case is cited here merely to dramatize the public nature of the corporation. Whether or not one condemns or praises corporate lobbying, its existence illustrates the often tight connection between major corporations and the process of government.

Corporations have, indeed, become an "important part of the process." The kinds of quasi-public activities described earlier under the categories of monopolies, externalities, and lobbying are so widespread and so integral to the corporation that many observers now view the traditional, libertarian view as inadequate and inaccurate as a descriptive theory. For many of the largest U.S. corporations it is no longer taken as self-evident that the very purpose of the organization is the maximization of profits for shareholders. This alternative view, which emphasizes the rights of employees, customers, local communities, and other groups with a legitimate interest in the corporation, has been labeled stakeholder theory. Evan and Freeman, in their pathfinding paper (1988), describe the theory as follows:

The concept of stakeholders is a generalization of the notion of stockholders, who themselves have some special claim on the firm. Just as stockholders have a right to demand certain actions by management, so do other stakeholders have a right to make claims. The exact nature of these claims is a difficult question that we shall address, but the logic is identical to that of the stockholder theory. Stakes require actions of a certain sort, and conflicting stakes require methods of resolution. (p. 149)

Similarly, Donaldson and Preston (1995), in reviewing the literature on stakeholder theory, summarize by noting that

the fundamental basis (of stakeholder theory) is *normative* and involves acceptance of the following ideas:

(a) Stakeholders are persons or groups with legitimate interests in procedural and/or substantive aspects of corporate activity. Stakeholders are identified by *their* interests in the corporation, whether the corporation has any corresponding functional interest in *them*.

(b) The interests of all stakeholders are of *intrinsic value*. That is, each group of stakeholders merits consideration for its own sake and not merely because of its ability to further the interests of some other group, such as the shareowners. (p. 67)

In other words, stakeholder theory not only describes the corporation as it exists but provides guidelines as to what the corporation potentially could and *should* be. "The theory is used to interpret the function of the corporation" (Donaldson and Preston, 1995, p. 71).

Although there still exist significant disagreements even among proponents of the stakeholder theory (Goodpaster, 1991, 1994), it should be noncontroversial that one of the great strengths of the theory is its accurate and forceful portrayal of the corporation as a public institution. One need not accept Christopher Stone's (1975) call for publicly appointed corporate board directors or the specific details of stakeholder theory to appreciate this point. The modern corporation is certainly something much more than the bounded, private world of corporate shareholders and managers.

The argument to this point suggests quite simply that corporations are to be classified, at least, as quasi-public institutions. This conclusion raises an important difficulty for those committed to both political liberalism and the possibility of a religiously grounded business ethics. For example, the right of employers in the quasi-public domain to discriminate in their hiring practices on the basis of sexual orientation cannot be equated with the right of a religious organization to do so. Greenawalt is correct when he notes that if an "employer is told that in hiring he may not discriminate against someone he believes is engaging in sinful practices, his religious liberty is implicated" (1988, p. 93). But what this analysis fails to factor in are the public aspects of the business corporation. The context in which the decision is made is crucial. Political liberalism would suggest that denying employment (or terminating employment) on the basis of sexual orientation is a possibility for purely private organizations. Obviously, such a possibility would be extremely problematic and difficult to defend in the public sphere. The original question of this chapter is now refined as follows: Is a religiously grounded business ethics, *an ethics appropriate for the quasi-public nature of the modern corporation*, consistent with the idea of political liberalism?

RELIGION IN THE PURELY PUBLIC SQUARE

Before turning specifically to the preceding question, a preliminary and more general question is raised, To what extent does political liberalism require a separation between religion and state? Robert Audi (1989) has recently presented a "framework that clarifies certain moral, legal, and political questions about religion and civil life" (p. 259). His theory is one of maximum separation and therefore serves as a proper location to begin this part of the discussion. Audi recognizes three broad doctrines, in his view, implicit in the general theory of separation of religion and state.

He labels the first set of principles "the institutional separation doctrine." Included here are the following three ideas:

A.1—The libertarian principle: The state must permit the practice of any religion. While not unlimited, this includes "freedom of religious belief," "freedom of worship," and "freedom to engage in the rites and rituals of one's religion."

A.2—The equalitarian principle: "The state may not give preference to one religion over another." (p. 263)

A.3—The neutrality principle: "The state should give no preference to religion (or religions) *as such*, that is, to institutions or persons simply because they are religious." (p. 264)

Each of these three principles is concerned primarily with the behavior of the government and can be justified, "given a commitment to a free and democratic society" (p. 262). The libertarian principle is intrinsic to the notion of democratic freedom at the heart of political liberalism, and its acceptance entails something like the equalitarian principle to support it. The neutrality principle is more complicated and controversial but is usually viewed as necessary to avoid political domination by the religious. These three principles provide the foundations for the notion of separation. The principles are thus extremely important but the least relevant for the present discussion, which is not primarily focused on the actions of the government per se. Audi's major contribution to the discussion can be found in the two additional doctrines he isolates.

Audi notes that for many of the same reasons that support the original doctrine cited earlier, religious groups like churches and synagogues should not interfere in matters of government. In other words, not only should the government pursue a policy of strict separation, but religion itself should intentionally restrict its activities and refrain from affecting important public matters. He carefully notes that this is an issue not of law but of voluntary morality. This insight leads him to formulate a second broad doctrine that he calls the "institutional principle of political neutrality." According to this principle,

B.1—"churches have a prima facie obligation to abstain from supporting candidates for office or pressing for specific public policies, especially the kind typically included in the platform of a particular party." (p. 274)

Audi immediately notes that this principle should not be taken to mean that churches and other religious groups must refrain from taking a "moral position" on public issues, but religious authorities need to remove completely all vestiges of religious influence.

Finally, Audi extends his theory to the individual citizen. This last extension, if valid, would have the broadest implications for those interested in a religiously grounded business ethics. This doctrine is called "principles of conscience." In this category, he includes two specific principles:

C.1—The principle of secular rationale: "in a free and democratic society, people who want to preserve religious and other liberties should not argue for or advocate laws or polices that restrict human conduct unless they offer (or at least have) adequate secular (nonreligious) reasons to support the law or policy in question." (p. 278)

C.2—The principle of secular motivation: "one should not advocate or promote any legal or public policy restrictions on human conduct unless one is . . . also motivated by adequate secular reason." (p. 284)

According to the principle of secular rationale, one might be opposed to polygamy on religious grounds, but one could support legal legislation to prohibit it only if one had a nonreligious reason for doing so, say the harm such a practice might cause children. The principle of secular motivation goes much further. Not only does it require the exclusive public use of secular reasoning, but it requires one to refrain from supporting restrictive legal legislation unless one is also motivated by purely secular reasoning. Motivation, traditionally conceived to be irrelevant for the theory of separation of religion and state, is here suddenly a significant determining variable.

Audi's position is an extreme one, especially if one keeps in mind that just about all government laws "restrict human conduct" in one way or another. To see how extreme his position is in the area of business ethics, we note that in response to a critique by Paul Weithman (1991), he insists that Catholic bishops, in fulfilling their "distinctively clerical obligations," should refrain from promoting "specific public policies" (Audi, 1991, p. 69). He allows that they are permitted to oppose economic injustice in a broad and general way. But he maintains they violated his separation theory when they made specific recommendations on the following issues: "job-training and apprenticeship programs, national eligibility standards for welfare programs, equitable pay for women, legislation extending labor protection to farm workers" (Weithman, 1991, p. 56). Audi is not stating that he disagrees with the position of the Catholic bishops on these issues but is making a much stronger claim. Political liberalism, he asserts, requires them not to formulate and communicate *any* stand at all.

Before rejecting Audi's position outright, it should be noted that even his maximalist position continues to recognize important roles, in terms of both inspiration and discovery, for a religiously grounded ethics (see p. 293).

Although one might be tempted to view this nod to the importance of religious "factors" as an afterthought and of no substantive import, this conclusion would be mistaken. While Audi's theory, in my opinion, does not go far enough in recognizing the legitimacy of religious language in the public sphere, his last point allows for a considerable degree of openness to a religious vocabulary. Consider the following trenchant critique of modern capitalism by Erich Fromm:

Alienation as we find it in modern society is almost total; it pervades the relationship of man to his work, to the things he consumes, to the state, to his fellow man, and to himself. Man has created a world of man-made things as it never existed before. He has constructed a complicated social machine to administer the technical machine he built. Yet this whole creation of his stands over and above him. He does not feel himself as a creator and center, but as the servant of a Golem, which his hands have built. The more powerful and gigantic the forces are which he unleashes, the more powerless he feels himself as a human being. He confronts himself with his own forces embodied in things he has created, alienated from himself. He is owned by his own creation, and has lost ownership of himself. He has built a golden calf, and says, "these are your gods who have brought you out of Egypt." (1955, p. 125)

Regardless of whether one agrees or not with Fromm's conclusion, is the form of this critique—with its free use of biblical and religious imagery and his invocation of the notion of idolatry—legitimate in a liberal democracy? Obviously, the answer is yes, and importantly for Audi, his theory would agree. Audi could argue that Fromm, far from advocating specific policies like a minimum wage, is engaged in a process of uncovering "new truths." His clear use of religious language and his citing of a specific biblical verse are meant to aid in discovery and inspiration. In fact, Fromm's critique is a partial antidote to Robert Allen's quote with which this chapter began.

Audi's position is extreme in its demand for separation, but, as the preceding indicates, it is not total. Nevertheless, Audi's view is subject to a number of important criticisms. Two bedrock assumptions underlying his approach are particularly troublesome. First, Audi defines secular reasoning simply as nonreligious reasoning. In his words, "a secular reason is, roughly, one whose normative force, that is, its status as a prima facie justificatory element, does not (evidentially) depend on the existence of God (for example, through appeals to divine command), or on theological considerations (such as interpretations of a sacred text), or on the pronouncements of a person or institution qua religious authority" (p. 278). The problem with such a definition, in the context of his paper, is that he is left with a view of all forms of reasoning as publicly acceptable, no matter how personal or idiosyncratic, except religious reasoning. Religious reasoning is distinguished from other comprehensive doctrines in that it alone is deemed unacceptable in the public sphere, where legislation restricting human conduct is concerned. Thus, one might be legitimately motivated by a Kantian or utilitarian ethic and act on the basis of such a comprehensive doctrine (knowing full well that others reject one's theoretical underpinnings), but not on the basis of a religious worldview. No justification for this important distinction is provided. This assumption is never defended in terms of an overall theory of political liberalism and clearly is inconsistent with Rawls' "freestanding" view mentioned earlier. It is patently unfair to single out arbitrarily religious language as the one comprehensive doctrine that is disallowed. As it stands, both Audi's institutional principle of political neutrality and his two principles of conscience are based on a dubious and never-defended distinction among comprehensive doctrines.

Second and more importantly, Audi's approach is ahistorical in the sense that his conclusions assume the existence of a perfectly just society. According to Audi, the political problem that his theory addresses is how to maintain the status quo, rather than how to create and to develop a just and stable society. This static assumption, although necessary for his strong conclusions, is clearly implausible as an accurate description of political realities. Weithman is correct when he defends the Catholic bishops' right to advocate specific public policies, based on "their belief that a well-functioning free democracy requires far greater economic justice than presently characterizes the U.S. economy. They also thought that an official and morally binding pronouncement by all the Bishops would best make members of their church understand and act upon their obligations of justice" (1991, pp. 56–57). Weithman extends his defense of religiously grounded political advocacy:

If the Bishops' goal—greater economic justice—is required by a commitment to democracy and if their advocacy of public policies in fact significantly helps to mobilize support for greater economic justice, it is at least not clear that they violated that moral obligation. (1991, p. 57)

Weithman also cogently defends religious institutional involvement in the Civil Rights movement in similar terms. If democracy demands racial equality, as it certainly does, then the attempt of religious leaders to help accelerate the process is an acceptable and perhaps even necessary activity in helping to create a just, pluralistic democracy. To suggest, as Audi does, that no circumstances justify religious involvement in the political process is too severe a condition. Democratic ideals include religious freedom and tolerance, but they also include issues related to economic justice and racial harmony. Some politically liberal societies, under certain conditions, may be willing to incur a loss of religious freedom to ensure a greater degree of economic justice. As economic justice in a society deteriorates, the likelihood of a positive contribution from religious institutions is greatly enhanced. That this trade-off is a difficult one to measure does not mean that it is always impossible to apply.

John Rawls' theory of political liberalism avoids Audi's unacceptable assumptions. Rawls' notion of separation is more moderate. His purposeful rejection of Audi's extreme assumptions helps to establish a more realistic and helpful theory of political liberalism that takes the possibility of the existence of religious truths as a live option more seriously. First, he does not arbitrarily single out religion for special treatment but views it as one among many reasonable, comprehensive doctrines. To the extent that religious language is excluded from the public sphere, so, too, are all references to any comprehensive doctrine. This is an important distinction between Audi and Rawls and should not be underestimated.

Second, Rawls does not require the exclusive use of public reasons for all political questions. The required use of public reasons is restricted only to those questions involving "constitutional essentials and questions of basic justice" (p. 214). Although Rawls is not always clear as to precisely what this includes or excludes, at least some legislation that restricts human conduct must be referred to in the following quote:

Many if not most political questions do not concern those fundamental matters, for example, much tax legislation and many laws regulating property; statutes protecting the environment and controlling pollution; establishing national parks and preserving wilderness areas and animal and plant species; and laying aside funds for museums and the arts. (1993, p. 214)

Rawls immediately qualifies this by noting that sometimes these issues do involve fundamental matters, but the essential point that, at least, some restrictive legislation can be supported through reference to a comprehensive doctrine (including religion) remains uncontested. To the extent that a religious business ethics is focused on "tax legislation" and "laws regulating property," it is, prima facie, consistent with political liberalism.

Finally, Rawls' theory is moderated in a third important way by his explicit recognition and identification of the "limits of public reason" (1993, p. 247). As against the "exclusive view" that specific reference to comprehensive doctrines can never be introduced into public reason on matters of fundamental concern, his theory suggests, consistent with Weithman, that "there is another view allowing citizens, in certain situations, to present what they regard as the basis of political values rooted in the comprehensive doctrine, provided they do this in ways that strengthen the ideal of public reason itself" (p. 247). This alternative view is labeled the "inclusive view." The distinction between the exclusive and inclusive views is made in explicit recognition that historical realities need to be factored into the analysis. The actually existing political circumstances determine the appropriate circumstances when reference to a comprehensive doctrine is acceptable. Rawls provides two concrete, historical examples in which public reliance on religious beliefs should be seen not only as tolerable but as necessary for the establishment of a just and democratic society. He states that abolitionists who opposed slavery as contrary to God's law as early as the 1830s provided a necessary force leading to the Civil War and the eventual eradication of slavery. "In this case the nonpublic reason of certain churches supported the clear conclusions of public reason" (1993, p. 250). Similarly, the successes of the Civil Rights movement of the 1960s are inextricably linked to the leadership of Martin Luther King, Jr. King's reliance on a religious vocabulary was not unreasonable in a politically liberal democracy scarred by racial injustice, and, in fact, his writings were "among the necessary historical conditions to establish political justice" (1993, pp. 250–251). In his justly famous "Letter from Birmingham City Jail," King himself links the religious values of the Judeo-Christian tradition to the democratic principles embedded in America's founding political documents. In defending his specific policy of nonviolent civil disobedience, King looks forward to the day when

the South will know that when these disinherited children of God sat down at lunch counters they were in reality standing up for the best in the American dream and the most sacred values in our Judeo-Christian heritage, and thusly, carrying our whole nation back to those great wells of democracy which were dug deep by the Founding Fathers in the formulation of the Constitution and the Declaration of Independence. (1963, p. 302)

Clearly, King's advocacy of specific public policies is motivated by his deep commitment to religious values and his attachment to political liberalism. King viewed religion and political liberalism as mutually supportive.

In summary, the theory of political liberalism can be understood in much more nuanced terms than at first suggested. Approaches that assume that citizens should attempt to observe a strict and complete separation between religiously grounded ethics and their public decisions are found wanting. Even the most extreme view of separation recognizes a role for religion in terms of both inspiration and discovery. Further, the more moderate and plausible stance of John Rawls suggests:

- Religion is excluded only to the extent that all comprehensive doctrines are excluded from the public debate.
- The use of public reason is restricted only to those questions involving constitutional essentials and questions of basic justice. Tax regulation and property law are excluded from this category.
- Finally, the rejection of the exclusive view in favor of the inclusive view is important in that it forcefully underscores the interdependency of politics and religion and thus opens up the possibility of an integration between them as demonstrated in the writings of Martin Luther King, Jr.

RELIGION IN THE QUASI-PUBLIC SQUARE

The preceding conclusions demonstrate unequivocally that political liberalism condones some reference to comprehensive doctrines, including religion, even with regard to purely public matters. As no one argues that business corporations must be more stringent than the state itself, and as there are no particularly strong reasons for suggesting otherwise, it follows directly that a religiously grounded business ethics is also potentially consistent with the idea of political liberalism. What remains to be shown are the desirability and need of a business ethics grounded in religious sources in the context of an emerging democratic polity.

Assuming the adequacy of Rawls' notion of political liberalism, one might recognize the right of individuals and businesses to invoke a religious view under certain restricted circumstances but might still maintain that there are no compelling reasons for doing so. Public reasons, appealing only to general beliefs and forms of reasoning found in common sense, and the noncontroversial methods and conclusions of science may provide a rich enough language to carry out the business ethics dialogue. This chapter rejects this thesis outright. Given the nature of business ethics and current historical realities, public reasons alone are inadequate. This is true for two distinct reasons.

First, the viability of business ethics depends upon a particular assumption about human beings' capabilities to take actions beyond what is dictated by purely self-interest calculations. As indicated later, the justification for making this assumption cannot be that it is a noncontroversial conclusion of science. Its acceptance, therefore, requires grounding in a comprehensive doctrine not necessarily shared by all members of a society. Second, a reliance on the exclusive use of public reasons leaves many important and vital issues unresolved or underdetermined. Religious guidance can, therefore, be an important basis for decision making in those cases where decisions must be taken.

Beyond Self-Interest

At its core, business ethics, like the theory of political liberalism, proposes that men and women are motivated by more than a complete reliance on self-interest. This proposition is pervasive in the business ethics literature. It is taken as self-evident that the business ethics climate will not be improved by teaching students to rely even more heavily on the self-interest model. Norman Bowie's explicit rejection of the self-interest model in favor of "the moral point of view" is typical. He writes in the very first issue of the *Business Ethics Quarterly*:

the main difference between the classic economic point of view and the moral point of view lay in the assumption by most economists that people behave egoistically while the business ethicist insists that people can—at least on occasion—behave non-egoistically. The economist accepts human preferences and the choices made on the basis of them (revealed preference theory) while the business ethicist serves to judge human preferences and the choices made on the basis of them. (1991, p. 3)

In the theory of political liberalism, Rawls calls the ability to move beyond pure egoism "reasonableness." "Persons are reasonable in one basic aspect when, among equals say, they are ready to propose principles and standards as fair terms of cooperation and to abide by them willingly, given the assurance that other will likewise do so" (1993, p. 49).

Business ethics, specifically, and political liberalism, more generally, rest entirely upon a particular view of what it means to be human. It assigns certain capabilities to its hypothetical business players and citizens. This ability, while accepted in many philosophical doctrines and most religions, is currently not part of what we might call public reasons, if by public reasons we restrict ourselves to the noncontroversial conclusions of science, and if by science we include the social sciences.

Many economists (some more forcefully than others), for example, explicitly reject the notion of reasonableness as even a possibility. Gary

Becker has provided the least apologetic formulation of the "anti-reasonableness doctrine":

I am saying that the economic approach provides a valuable unified framework for understanding *all* human behavior. . . . The heart of my argument is that human behavior is not compartmentalized, sometimes based on maximizing, sometimes not, sometimes motivated by stable preferences, sometimes by volatile ones, sometimes resulting in an optimal accumulation of information, sometimes not. Rather, all human behavior can be viewed as involving participants who maximize their utility from a stable set of preferences and accumulate an optimal amount of information and other inputs in a variety of markets. (Becker, 1976, p. 14)

In plain English, Becker believes human agents are always pure egoists and never reasonable. This scientific thesis supposedly holds whether agents will admit it to themselves or not. Among some of the implications Becker draws from this starting point is the conclusion that real corporate social responsibility, where managers specify clear environmental, consumer, employee, and community goals (Johnson & Johnson's famous credo provides a good example), is impossible (if not a meaningless construct). Managerial talk about corporate social responsibility is fully explained by the profit maximization motive and should be understood as an attempt on the part of business leaders to avoid public intervention in the marketplace (see 1976, p. 12). Becker's diluted notion of corporate social responsibility is thus very different from Norman Bowie's vision. The clarity of Becker's view, the creativity and ingenuity with which he supports it, and its nearly universal acceptance among economists suggest that a broader debate between economists and ethicists is called for. I still suspect that Rawls is correct in describing rational agents as nearly "psychopathic" when they exclusively pursue self-interest, but the clear articulation of the antireasonableness doctrine and its apparent widespread acceptance demand recourse to more broad-based, comprehensive doctrines. Given current historical realities and the current intellectual climate, a serious business ethics cannot be built exclusively upon public reasons. Rather, at the present time, especially given the predominant assumption of economists, business ethics requires a basic assumption about human capabilities that requires invoking comprehensive doctrines that are not necessarily accepted by all members of society as noncontroversial. One cannot yet justify reasonableness by appealing only to scientific findings or to "general beliefs and forms of reasoning found in common sense."

Religious sources, including biblical narratives and specific moral teachings, provide deep support for the existence of the kinds of human characteristics necessary for building a reasonable and practical business ethics. The argument is not that religious sources exclusively provide such teachings, but religious sources, among other comprehensive doctrines, are potentially necessary. Human beings committed to a religious way of life are often convinced, in part, because of the satisfying and meaningful life that they personally experience, that it is sensible to talk about reasonableness as a human motivation. This does not mean that these people can prove or even communicate this belief in a convincing way to nonbelievers with knockdown arguments. But it does suggest that if invoked carefully and appropriately, religious business ethics, far from being inconsistent with political liberalism, can actually strengthen it. Using Rawls' terminology, the last suggestion calls for the inclusive use of religious language to support democratic ideals.

In the Jewish tradition, with which I am most familiar, three modern religious thinkers come to mind immediately in this context. The writings of Joseph Soloveitchik (1965, 1967, 1983), Abraham Joshua Heschel (1951, 1955, 1965), and Will Herberg (1951)—orthodox, conservative, and reform, respectively—although in many respects very different in both form and substance, provide models of how to integrate religious teachings with assumptions of pluralistic societies. While none of these luminaries dealt specifically with business ethics per se, their writings demonstrate the power and place of authentic religious values in support of democratic ideals. Each of these religious leaders, in his own unique way, recognized the necessity to reach beyond public reasons in support of political liberalism.

Filling the Gaps

Free and equal citizens are the basic building blocks of a just and stable society. Political participants and businesspeople should make an honest attempt to solve allocation problems within both the state and the modern corporation by restricting themselves to the use of public reasons when justifying restrictive policies in the public sphere. In this way, they demonstrate their sincere beliefs in the dignity and equality of human beings. Citizens recognize the existence of competing, but reasonable, comprehensive doctrines, but for political purposes they self-consciously restrict themselves to language that is comprehensible to all (public reasons). Political liberalism is, above all, a practical enterprise, attempting to explain the possibility of establishing and maintaining pluralistic societies.

Fully endorsing the preceding paragraph, it remains true that some public issues cannot yet (and perhaps may never) be resolved by divorcing ourselves completely from comprehensive doctrines. Simplifying, the exclusive use of public reasons leaves too many gaps.

Kent Greenawalt (1988, 1990) has examined and defended this thesis extensively. Summarizing his view, he writes:

Legislation must be justified in terms of secular objectives, but when people reasonably think that shared premises of justice and criteria for determining truth cannot resolve critical questions of fact, fundamental questions of value, or the weighing of competing benefits and harms, they do appropriately rely on religious convictions that help them answer these questions. Not only is such reliance appropriate for ordinary citizens, legislators in similar instances may also rely on their own religious convictions and those of their constituents, and occasionally such reliance is warranted even for judges. Though reliance on religious convictions may be appropriate in these settings, argument in religious terms is often an inapt form of public dialogue. (1988, p. 12)

Three points deserve emphasis here. First, Greenawalt endorses fully a notion of political liberalism. Second, he suggests that reasonable people will agree that in certain situations questions of facts and values will be subject to the "choice" of comprehensive doctrines. Third, in reminding us that "argument in religious terms is often an inapt form of public dialogue," he implicitly suggests that a "translation" from the language of comprehensive doctrine to public reasons is both possible and necessary. This means that one can be motivated to promote a particular policy primarily by examining and interpreting one's religious beliefs but openly justify the proposed policy in terms of public reasons only. There is nothing sinister about this process as long as the process itself is publicly recognized and accepted. This is not to suggest that the translation will correspond one-to-one. Translations from one language to another are never literal, but they can serve practical purposes. To reject translation because it fails to convey certain nuances of the original is an impossible and quixotic criterion.

Greenawalt identifies a number of specific issues where public reasons alone are insufficient for arriving at convincing conclusions. Among other issues, he discusses animal rights, abortion, and environmental policies. His discussion of welfare assistance touches most closely on business ethics concerns. After examining alternative welfare policies, including what he calls hands-off and interventionist policies, he concludes:

Common reasoning cannot settle whether individuals have any basic moral right to the fruits of their talents and if so exactly how far that right should be curbed or qualified in the interests of general welfare. As with other issues we have examined, premises beyond public reasons must determine choices among a number of plausible competitors. (1988, p. 182)

The public reasons gap explored here provides a second important rationale for an endorsement of religious business ethics. Consider each of the following questions related to business ethics:

- What are the potential conflicts inherent between the goals of business firms and the environment? How are these conflicts to be decided?
- Should managers screen investments using ethical criteria in addition to traditional financial criteria?
- What are the firm's responsibilities toward employees? Specifically, how do corporations resolve conflicts about (1) employee autonomy and empowerment, (2) discrimination, (3) employee training, (4) responsibilities toward the unemployed, and (5) hiring, promotion, and termination issues?
- To what extent is the profit motive an acceptable goal of the business enterprise? Is the emerging stakeholder model (described briefly earlier) ethically more acceptable than the profit maximization view?

No consensus has emerged on any of these or related questions. As with the welfare issue, public reasons alone cannot provide a realistic, practical business ethics appropriate for the modern corporation. Religiously grounded business ethics and business ethics grounded on other comprehensive doctrines legitimately provide answers to some of these questions. (From a Jewish perspective, see Levine and Pava, 1999.) If these answers (1) promote the ideals of political liberalism (by respecting the requirements of pluralism), (2) are viewed as universal in scope (all human beings in similar circumstance are treated alike), and (3) are treated as noncoercive (the answers are compelling in and of themselves and do not require specific beliefs about religious authority), then they are fully appropriate as justifications for the promotion of specific business policies.

Religious Business Ethics as a Three-Step Process

Following the preceding analysis, religious business ethics can be thought of as a three-step process. In the first phase of the process, the attempt is made to answer specific questions by invoking public reasons only. In this way, potentially controversial propositions are completely avoided. In restricting oneself to common sense and universally accepted scientific conclusions, all reasonable human beings can be expected to endorse the answers. The higher the percentage of issues dealt with in this way, the better, even from the perspective of any given comprehensive doctrine. This is true because, by definition, the resulting policy will be consistent with all reasonable, comprehensive doctrines.

In this first phase, in those instances where a proactive policy cannot be defended by the use of public reasons, one might seriously consider if there is some way to avoid making a public decision altogether, especially if the issue touches on constitutional essentials and questions of basic justice. At the level of the state, for example, some have argued that a public policy granting women the right to choose an abortion is a way for the polity to refrain essentially from making any decision at all. This has been called the "liberty principle." It asserts that "if a judge cannot resolve a case on the basis of publicly available reasons, then the judge must preserve liberty, usually deciding for the defendant and leaving the moral choice to individuals or voluntary communities" (Solum, 1990, p. 1102). While I believe that this principle is inappropriate to abortion concerns, as it ignores the "potential" liberty of the fetus, it may have wide application in the area of business ethics. One example where the liberty principle is properly invoked is in our attitude toward the marketing and use of tobacco products. A unique feature of the cigarette is that it is a product that, when used properly, significantly increases the likelihood of serious illness and even death. Nevertheless, public reasoning alone cannot justify its outright prohibition, and the liberty principle appropriately calls for leaving the moral choice to the individual to the extent that this is possible.

The second phase of the process is necessary only if it has been determined that some public decision must be made, and public reasoning is insufficient to ground a policy decision. At this phase, one looks back to one's comprehensive doctrine to determine if it contains an answer (it is often assumed, as the name implies, that comprehensive doctrines have answers to all ethically significant questions). The answer will necessarily be dependent on specific assumptions of the comprehensive doctrine and therefore will be incomprehensible (at least to some extent) to those who do not share the doctrine.

This phase of the process requires a stepping back, as it were, and an immersion in one's own comprehensive doctrine. Even if it is assumed that the comprehensive doctrine contains answers to all ethically significant questions, this phase of the process is often wrongly caricatured as moralistic, mechanical, and unthinking (De George, 1986). A better way of conceiving this aspect of the process is as "interpretation." Interpretation is not merely a handing down of traditional institutions and texts from one generation to the next. Interpretation is the process of taking ownership of the texts and, in turn, the ethical world. Interpretation is thus, in part, a humanly creative process (Pava, 1997).

The third phase, often formally overlooked, requires a process of translation. An attempt is made to justify the specific policy—motivated by a specific comprehensive doctrine—in the most comprehensible and understandable way possible. Translation is a necessary step if actual deliberation is to lead to some sort of resolution. As Amy Gutmann explains:

The give and take of respectful argument among people with conflicting reasonable perspectives is a fairer way of living with ongoing disagreement for several reasons. It enjoins the respect that is due to all reasonable opinions without assuming that the provisional resolution of a fundamental moral conflict can be politically neutral in its rationale or result. Mutually respectful people are open to the possibility of changing their minds in the light of unanswerable objections to their present point of view, and they thereby increase the chances of collectively discovering a just resolution that is presently unseen. Even in the absence of such discovery, the give and take of respectful argument can create the broadest justifiable consensus across a range of reasonable but conflicting positions because mutual respect enjoins an economy of moral disagreement, the search for substantive points of convergence between fundamentally irreconcilable positions. (1993, pp. 198–199)

Gutmann calls this process "deliberative universalism." But if the benefits of the process are to accrue, translation must play an integral and central role. The translation is done openly and honestly and is attempted in full recognition of the fact that it will require an explanation of assumptions unique to one's own comprehensive doctrine. The point is not necessarily to convince others working out of alternative doctrines (although this may be a happy result) of the ultimate truth of one's position but to allow others to examine and understand one's reasoning.

It remains true that translations are never literal, but the process is beneficial both to the policy advocate forced by the circumstance to work within a specific comprehensive doctrine and to the affected parties. Rather than thinking of translations as bridges, think of them as a set of directions. "Starting from a specific location I arrived here by taking the following route." Those engaged in the process of translation will benefit by carefully reexamining conclusions and the process by which those conclusions were arrived at. Those affected or potentially affected by the policies will be brought closer to an understanding of why a particular policy is advocated. Even where disagreement arises, translations allow for a minimum level of communication and symbolize a deep respect for the possibility of a civil dialogue.

CONCLUSION

The contemporary Jewish philosopher David Hartman has given us hope that a rapprochement between religion and political liberalism is possible.

If we can assume that it is possible for individuals to agree on what they reject, without acknowledging what they affirm, we may be able to create a shared theology of the repudiation of idolatry, without demanding a clearly defined commitment to belief in God. The believer can share common aspirations with the atheist and the agnostic, if all three strive to reject idolatry. This striving can have great significance and far-ranging consequences if the idolatry that is combated is luring, and constitutes a vital problem to be eradicated. (1978, p. 147)

Nevertheless, many religious thinkers are wedded, a priori, to a view that the relationship between religion and political liberalism is necessarily an antagonistic one. Similarly, many secular thinkers reject the notion that religion can play any kind of positive role in the development of strong, democratic societies. This chapter is directed to everyone else who remains intellectually curious and open to the possibilities that (1) a democratic society can be strengthened by religion, (2) religion can be strengthened in a democratic society, and (3) the integration of democracy and religion is a potentially important experiment. These remarks hold at the level of both the purely public, where to date they have received the most attention, and the quasi-public modern corporation.

The religiously sanctioned humanistic attitude reflected here is best captured in the Jewish sources by the biblical phrase, "It is not in heaven." The rabbis' interpretation of these words is most famously expressed in the following Talmudic tale. Rabbi Eliezer ben Hyrcanus, one of the most important rabbinic scholars in the period after the destruction of the second Temple, disagreed with the majority of sages about a particular point of law. Rabbi Eliezer declared the oven of "Akhnai" ritually pure (and thus fit for use), while the sages ruled it impure (and not fit for use). More important than the specific details of this case are the events surrounding its ultimate resolution. After describing the disagreement, the Talmud continues:

It has been taught: "On that day, Rabbi Eliezer used all the arguments in the world, but they did not accept [them] from him. He said to them: 'If the *Halakhah* is in accordance with me, let this carob tree prove [it].' The carob tree was uprooted from its place one hundred cubits—and some say four hundred cubits. They said to him: 'One does not bring proof from a carob tree.' He said to them: 'If the *Halakhah* is in accordance with me, let the channel of water prove [it].' The channel of water turned backward. They said to him: 'One does not bring proof from a channel of water.' He then said to them: 'If the *Halakhah* is in accordance with me, let the walls of the House of Study prove [it].' The walls of the House of Study leaned to fall. Rabbi Yehoshua rebuked them, [and] said to them: 'If Talmudic Sages argue with one another about the *Halakhah*, what affair is it of yours?' They did not fall, out of respect for Rabbi Yehoshua; but they did not straighten out, out of respect for Rabbi Eliezer, and they still remain leaning. He then said to them: 'If the *Halakhah* is in accordance with me, let it be proved from Heaven.' A [heavenly] voice went forth and said: 'Why are you [disputing] with Rabbi Eliezer, for the Halakhah is in accordance with him everywhere?' Rabbi Yehoshua rose to his feet and said: 'It is not in heaven.' " (Bava Metzia 59b)

The incredible conclusion of this story is that even when God himself intervenes, the sages do not listen—"It is not in heaven." As in the image in Ronald Dworkin's (1985; see pp. 158) chain novel, the rabbis understood their unique role as extending the previous chapters in the best possible way. A postscript to the story adds that when God saw Rabbi Yehoshua get up and quote the written Torah, against God's own view, "The Holy One, blessed be He . . . smiled and said: 'My sons have defeated Me, My sons have defeated me' " (Bava Metzia 59b). One is cautioned and sobered by the still leaning walls of the study house. But, ultimately, Rabbi Yehoshua's response and declaration are the only correct point of departure for later generations. To appreciate the power of Rabbi Yehoshua's words, contrast them with Robert Allen's justification for eliminating 40,000 employees—"I don't make the rules."

7

Can Business Ethics
Be Measured?

Few corporations claim to promote "meaning" explicitly, and none attempt to measure it. Nevertheless many, if not most, major U.S. and international corporations pledge allegiance, in some way or another, to business ethics and the notion of corporate social responsibility. For example, even a cursory examination of a random sample of annual reports indicates the existence of at least some disclosures of corporate social responsibility activities. Preston (1981), for example, concluded that well over half of the *Fortune* 500 companies presented some social disclosure material in the annual report to shareholders. More recently, Pava and Krausz (1995, 1998) presented evidence that suggests that not only do companies report about social responsibility activities on an ad hoc basis, but, more optimistically, there exists a positive statistical relationship between perceived corporate social responsibility by outside stakeholders and corporate disclosures in the "President's Letter to Shareholders." Yet, in spite of the existence of verbal disclosures and relatively general statements about meeting corporate social responsibilities, little quantitative data are supplied by U.S. corporations to aid investors and other interested parties in evaluating such claims. There is more than just a kernel of truth in Robert Kaplan and David Norton's recent observation about the need for quantification. The authors, echoing Lord Kelvin's dictum, write, "Measurement matters: if you can't measure it, you can't manage it" (1996, p. 21). Unquestionably, one of the great disappointments for the business ethics movement is the lack of successful measures (and the public disclosure of such measures when they do exist) in the area of corporate social responsibility. How well is a company performing in terms of business ethics and corporate social responsibility? From a stakeholder perspective, it will continue to be difficult to answer this question until business develops, implements, and publicizes relevant, reliable, comparable, nontraditional social responsibility measures.

The traditional financial and managerial accounting systems are under increasing attack from a number of different perspectives. The charged and highly emotional atmosphere at a recent conference jointly sponsored by New York University's Law School and Stern School of Business, marking the 25th anniversary of the Financial Accounting Standards Board (the private sector group in charge of establishing accounting rules in the United States), reflects the increasing discomfort with the venerable, double-entry accounting model (June 11–12, 1998). For the accounting profession, "business as usual" is becoming an increasingly difficult goal to defend. More and more, traditional accounting methods are thought to be beside the point, or worse.

Leif Edvinsson and Michael Malone, among many others, have recently pointed out how the current financial accounting environment often provides a disincentive for corporate managers to innovate and implement cutting-edge strategies. Research and development costs, investments in human resources, and reorganization costs all take a chunk out of current income under current generally accepted accounting principles (GAAP). Rather than calling these investments assets as corporate managers surely do (why else would they engage in these activities unless they expected increased future cash flows?), the Financial Accounting Standards Board (FASB) requires companies to write off these costs to income as incurred. Why don't more companies choose innovative strategies? According to Edvinsson and Malone:

To implement many of them would in fact hurt the company's books in the short term thanks to the cost of reorganization, buying MIS [management information systems] equipment, improving customer service systems, putting in place electronic data interchange systems with suppliers, establishing a strategic planning operation, and so on. Down the line these actions may make the company's books look rosy indeed, but for the near term they make those same books appear weak against shortsighted competitors who maintain the status quo—and that in turn will compromise the company's ability to obtain capital. Simply put, the smart, forward-looking company is punished for trying to maintain its competitiveness and earnings capability. (1997, pp. 30–31)

Edvinsson and Malone believe that GAAP may actually hurt, rather than help strengthen, the economy. The traditional accounting model "ultimately retards the entire economy's ability to maintain its competitiveness in rapidly changing environments" (p. 31). Given current accounting rules, good managers who want to get a fair hearing from the public must convince financial analysts and corporate shareholders to ignore quarterly reports that appear excessively negative. Financial reports that should convey information in an unbiased way are often unduly conservative in practice. Something has gone wrong.

The underlying complaint against accounting is that as the business environment has changed dramatically in the last quarter century, neither financial nor managerial accounting has kept pace. Robert K. Elliott described the situation as follows:

Information technology (IT) is changing everything. It represents a new, post-industrial paradigm of wealth creation that is replacing the industrial paradigm and is profoundly changing the way business is done. Because of these changes in business, the decisions that management must make are very different from former decisions. If the purpose of accounting information is to support business decision-making, and management's decision types are changing, then it is natural to expect accounting to change—both internal and external accounting. (Elliott, 1992, p. 61)

One way to get a feel for the magnitude of the problem described by Elliott is to examine the relationship between market values of stockholders' equity and book values of stockholders' equity for the five largest U.S. industrial corporations. The market values are determined by multiplying the price per share of the company by total number of outstanding shares. Market value, in a relatively efficient market like the U.S. stock market, captures the underlying economic value of the company. The market value represents the public's best estimate of the intrinsic value of the net assets of the corporation. The book value, by contrast, is an accounting number derived from the company's balance sheet. It is also an estimate of the net assets of the company, but it is an estimate based on the traditional financial accounting model (GAAP) and not investors' best estimates.

The following table indicates, for example, that General Motors has a market value nearly three times as great as its book value (298 percent), Wal-Mart has a market value of more than six times its book value (615 percent), and General Electric has a market value of more than seven and a half times book value (755 percent). Or, to put it in slightly different terms, for every dollar of net assets the accountants are currently including, on average (for all five of the companies in the table), the market sees $4.55. These data show that while accountants may (or may not be) reliably measuring those assets that they are attempting to measure, they are measuring only a small subset of what the market believes are the true economic resources of the corporation. Ignoring assets related to research and development, human resources, goodwill, reputation, trust, brand images, and so on is making accounting balance sheets relatively useless to savvy investors. The large and growing gap between market values and book values is staggering. If balance sheets are to play a role in the emerging knowledge economy, accountants must attempt to measure the growing number of intangible assets, as well as the tangible assets. Care must be taken to develop reliable measures, but too often the lack of reliability is used as an excuse to do nothing rather than innovate creatively.

Company Size	Company	Market Value to Book Value
1	General Motors	298%
2	Ford	241%
3	Exxon	364%
4	Wal-Mart Stores	615%
5	General Electric	755%
	Average	**455%**

A MODEST PROPOSAL: LEGITIMATE TRANSPARENCY

Perhaps, the problem with accounting is that we're asking it to do too much, especially those of us asking for increased social responsibility. Turning specifically to the question of this chapter, Can business ethics be measured?, perhaps the answer is no or, at best, not yet. There continue to be too many disagreements about what exactly does and does not constitute ethical and socially responsible business behavior. In view of this observation, this chapter suggests that a practical role for accounting begins with the modest recognition that the primary goal of the measurement system is *legitimate transparency*—not *evaluation*. Simply put, this means that stakeholders should have access to all information to which they are entitled. Stakeholders can engage in ethical and moral evaluation only to the extent that information about corporate activities and impacts is made publicly available. The important point here is that one has to carefully disentangle the measurement and disclosure functions from everything else. First disclose; then let others (both insiders and outsiders) judge. Ultimately, the accounting system should explicitly reveal the corporate story but should suppress overly pious attempts at identifying the "moral" of the story. End users of the system should be supplied with sufficient details of plot and character to devise their own moral. Here, Henry James' novels provide a better metaphor than Aesop's fables.

The overriding goal of any type of measuring device is to disclose particular characteristics, not to make value judgments about those characteristics. One doesn't want a scale that measures human weight to insult and criticize overweight users.

To some, legitimate transparency as the goal of the measuring system may seem so obvious as to border on the tautological. After all, what else can a measuring stick do but measure? The truth is, however, that, increasingly, accounting is viewed as one more tool in management's arsenal. Rather than being viewed as a neutral measuring system, accounting is being reconceived as a strategic weapon to maximize shareholder wealth. This is a dangerous change.

One can't help but wonder out loud whether or not Sunbeam's recent questionable accounting practices are related to its former chief executive officer's notorious macho corporate philosophy. "Chainsaw" Albert J. Dunlap (he was also affectionately described as "Rambo in pinstripes") was the darling of the business media with his insistence that the only thing that really mattered was the bottom line. The title of his book, *Mean Business*, colorfully captured his underlying core beliefs. At Sunbeam, Dunlap fired half the workers and closed more than half its facilities. But what apparently worked at a series of other companies didn't work quite as well at Sunbeam. Did Al Dunlap's aggressive business philosophy create an environment where accounting irregularities flourished? If leadership is constantly proclaiming that the only thing that matters is short-term stock market performance, might this lead to the belief that even accounting should be made to bow exclusively to shareholder interests? The Securities and Exchange Commission is now investigating (*New York Times*, June 26, 1998). Less than one year after reporting remarkable revenue growth, the company's inventories are mounting almost as fast as the stock price is dropping.

The call for legitimate transparency is not meant to put an end to the debate about what kinds of information should be disclosed or not. In fact, just the opposite. We need more discussion about this issue, not less. Accounting expert Baruch Lev is surely correct when he writes in a response to an earlier criticism by Pava and Krausz (1994) that it is impossible to disclose "all" potentially relevant information to every stakeholder.

Consider, for example, an oil company which discovered after an extensive and costly exploration a significant oil field. To recoup the heavy exploration costs and provide reasonable return to investors and long-term employment prospects to its employees, the company must acquire additional tracts of land adjacent to the explored field. However, if the oil find is publicly announced, the price of this land will skyrocket rendering the entire investment questionable. (Lev, 1994, p. 140)

I agree that some information is proprietary—stakeholders should have access to all information to which they are entitled, but they are not necessarily entitled to all information. In this case the oil company has a right to purchase the adjacent land at prevailing market prices (which do not reflect the oil find). What this case does not support, however, is Lev's emphatic call for managers to increasingly view disclosure decisions as one more opportunity to advance corporate interests. This is the antithesis to the notion of legitimate transparency. Consider the same oil company as it transports oil over public waterways and chooses to use a substandard vessel and therefore unilaterally imposes high risks on hundreds, if not thousands, of noncontracting third parties. Here legitimate transparency would surely argue for more disclosure rather than less, regardless of the results of management's own cost-benefit calculations. If the accounting function is to be useful to anyone at all, there needs be at least the possibility that it will require managers to measure and disclose information—even when they don't want to.

Intel's recent opposition to a shareholder resolution to enter into a dialogue with the Coalition for Environmentally Responsible Economics (CERES) and to consider adopting the CERES principles (originally called the Valdez principles when first introduced in 1989), in spite of the fact that almost 10 percent of shareholders favored the resolution (an extremely high percentage for a first-time resolution of this sort), is hardly a step forward for the company. Intel was ranked 82nd out of 100 in a study sponsored by the United Nations Environment Program measuring corporate environmental reporting. The CERES principles were originally written to encourage voluntary corporate commitment to environmental progress. The ten principles include protection of the biosphere, sustainable use of natural resources, reduction and disposal of waste, energy conservation, risk reduction, safe products and services, environmental restoration, informing the public, management commitment, audits, and reports. In fact, CERES companies must agree to complete a standardized, annual reporting format that is tied directly to the principles.

In spite of this and other setbacks, the call for increased transparency is not quixotic. Unlike Intel, ITT Industries has recently joined an increasing number of major corporations that have endorsed the CERES principles (General Motors, Sun, Coca-Cola, Domino's Pizza, Polaroid, Ben and Jerry's, H. B. Fuller, and United States Trust Company of Boston, among many others, previously all endorsed CERES principles). ITT Industries with nearly $9 billion in revenue during 1997 makes automotive parts, defense and aerospace electronics, and fluid-handling products. Usha Wright, vice president of environment, safety, and health for the company, defended management's decision as follows: "Our system of stating our objectives, measuring performance, auditing our operations and reporting our progress will help us fulfill our overall goal of leadership in the area of environmental responsibility" (ITT Industries Press Release, February 24, 1997).

The best U.S. companies strive to achieve legitimate transparency. The annual reports of Warren Buffett's Berkshire Hathaway are models of clarity, precision, and full disclosure. These reports attempt to convey a wide assortment of corporate information in a neutral and unbiased way. "Buffett tells it like it is, or at least as he sees it. That quality attracts an interested shareholder constituency to Berkshire, which flocks to its annual meetings in increasing numbers every year. Unlike what happens at most annual shareholder meetings, a sustained and productive dialogue on business issues results," according to legal scholar Lawrence Cunningham (1997, p. 8).

Consider Berkshire Hathaway's report on "Shareholder-Designated Contributions," included as part of the corporate annual report (available on-line at www.berkshirehathaway.com). Buffett carefully describes the corporation's core beliefs on corporate philanthropy. According to the document, managers, on a case-by-case basis, will unilaterally determine which donations will benefit the company either directly or indirectly. However, the total dollar amount of such giving is usually quite low. For the most part, Berkshire Hathaway's significant corporate giving ($15,424,480 to more than 3,800 charities in 1997—as clearly communicated in the report) is determined directly by shareholder preferences.

Each Berkshire shareholder—on a basis proportional to the number of shares of Berkshire that he owns—will be able to designate recipients of charitable contributions by our company. You'll name the charity; Berkshire will write the check. . . .

Just as I wouldn't want you to implement your personal judgments by writing checks on my bank account for charities of your choice, I feel it's inappropriate to write checks on your corporate "bank account" for charities of my choice. Your charitable preferences are as good as mine and, for both you and me, funds available to foster charitable interests in a tax-deductible manner reside largely at the corporate level rather than in our own hands. (Berkshire Hathaway, Annual Report, 1997)

The point is not that all shareholders and other interested parties will agree with Warren Buffett's investment strategies and corporate policies. As explicitly stated before, stakeholders continue to disagree about the precise contours of corporate social responsibility. Many shareholders, for example, might still strongly prefer no corporate charity whatsoever, or perhaps an even more liberal policy on corporate giving. Buffett's attempt at transparency (his clear description and defense of the policy) is a sufficient and adequate response to such demands. Legitimate transparency is a key to building ethical organizations, both for-profit and not-for-profit.

THE BALANCED SCORECARD: A STEP IN THE RIGHT DIRECTION

Robert Kaplan and David Norton's innovative notion of the "balanced scorecard" represents a positive move toward building increasingly ethical corporations, even if the authors almost certainly would either be indifferent to this observation or distance themselves from it. If the goal of the organization's accounting system is transparency, then implementing something like the balanced scorecard is surely a first step in the right direction. The following quote suggests the flavor of the balanced scorecard:

Information age companies will succeed by investing in and managing intellectual assets. . . . As organizations invest in acquiring these new capabilities, their success (or failure) cannot be motivated or measured by the traditional financial accounting model. . . .

The Balanced Scorecard is a new framework for integrating measures derived from strategy. While retaining financial measures of past performance, the Balanced Scorecard introduces the drivers of future financial performance. The drivers, encompassing customer, internal-business process, and learning and growth perspectives, are derived from an explicit and rigorous translation of the organization's strategy into tangible objectives and measures. (p. 18)

Consistent with the observations in the preceding section, Kaplan and Norton are insistent that the business environment has dramatically changed. Mass production and standard products are icons of the bygone industrial age. Postindustrial businesses—the information-age companies—recognize that the most important assets are intangible and intellectual in nature; they reside primarily in the minds of men and women working for the organization; you can't touch or feel these assets, but they are just as economically real as the buildings and factories in which the employees do their thinking. The accounting problem is to make these intangible assets tangible. As the authors write, traditional accounting systems are backward-looking—the balanced scorecard with its emphasis on integrating the "drivers of future financial performance" into a single report, by contrast, looks toward tomorrow and beyond.

Each balanced scorecard is different. Nevertheless, the authors contend that most of them will contain most of the following core outcome measures:

Core Financial Measures

- Return-on-investment
- Profitability
- Revenue growth/mix
- Cost reduction productivity

Core Customer Measures

- Market share
- Customer acquisition
- Customer retention
- Customer profitability
- Customer satisfaction

Core Learning and Growth Measures

• Employee satisfaction

• Employee retention

• Employee productivity (Kaplan and Norton, 1996, p. 306)

In addition, managers devise performance drivers (distinct from outcome measures) in each of these areas. These drivers are designed to predict the preceding outcome measures in a clear, understandable, and timely manner. These drivers are unique to industry and company. Ultimately, the balanced scorecard is not merely an ad hoc collection of measures but "should be the translation of the business unit's strategy into a linked set of measures that define both the long-term strategic objectives, as well as the mechanisms for achieving those objectives" (Kaplan and Norton, 1996, p. 32). To some extent, it's even fair to say that the balanced scorecard is to the organization what self-consciousness is to the individual.

Even as I praise the balanced scorecard, Kaplan and Norton are careful to distance themselves from the business ethics and social responsibility literature. For example, Kaplan and Norton challenged managers at a chemical company who wanted to include environmental compliance measures as part of the balanced scorecard, arguing that environmental compliance will not produce "competitive advantage." Kaplan and Norton were convinced that environmental compliance was important enough to include in the balanced scorecard only after managers at the chemical company explicitly explained to them how outstanding environmental and community performance was a central part of that company's strategy to increase long-run profits (see p. 35). Kaplan and Norton do not entertain the possibility that managers may possess environmental and community responsibilities even in the absence of any direct linkage to corporate strategy and that such responsibilities may even constitute a key element of the corporation's core vision (as an unbiased reading of most corporate credos seems to suggest; see Abrahams, 1995).

Nevertheless, their book is a primary resource to begin to understand how to increase the transparency of the modern organization, both for-profit and not-for-profit. Kaplan and Norton take an admittedly fuzzy concept, legitimate transparency, and begin to mechanize it and make it more useful. For this reason, even if one does not accept the foundational assumptions of their approach—that the ultimate goal of the corporation is the maximization of corporate profits—one can continue to view their book as a major advance, if not a breakthrough, in the practice and theory of measuring and communicating corporate activity.

My optimism stems from the underlying belief that the balanced scorecard can be (and will be) ultimately unplugged from the authors' continued insistence that the sole goal of the business enterprise is maximization of profits for corporate shareholders. The authors' observation that "the opportunity for the scorecard to improve the management of governmental and not-for-profit enterprises is even greater" than for the private sector (p. 179) lends strong credence to this belief. In fact, my intuition is that implementing and using a balanced scorecard, or something like it, will eventually alter managers' own beliefs about corporate goals. I say this for the simple reason that increased self-consciousness is almost always associated with a more nuanced understanding of underlying goals and aspirations, at the individual level or at the corporate level. In this case, it's hard to believe that a corporation measuring things like employee retention and satisfaction, customer satisfaction, product quality, factory safety, and environmental performance will not eventually come to understand these numbers not only as means to an end (shareholder profits) but also as legitimate ends in themselves.

Even Kaplan and Norton seem to let down their guard, if for just a moment, when they happily point out that the balanced scorecard, unlike conventional reengineering programs, does not lead to a "slash and burn strategy" (1996, p. 14). They put this in parentheses to be sure, but it is, at least, seemingly included as a recognized benefit of the balance scorecard in and of itself. Finally, it's fair to guess that Kaplan and Norton themselves—at least toward the end of the book—may have come to the conclusion that the scorecard can be transformative. They write: "This articulation of how individual tasks align with overall business unit objectives has created *intrinsic motivation* among large numbers of organizational employees. Their innovation and problem-solving energies have become unleashed, even without explicit ties to compensation incentive" (p. 21; emphasis added).

At the heart of the balanced scorecard approach is an intriguing and captivating vision of corporate life. It is a vision that vigorously and unapologetically introduces the notion of corporate ambiguity and the hope for corporate learning. What is the best metaphor to help understand organizational life?

The metaphor is closer to that of sailing in a highly competitive race, under changing weather and sea conditions, than that of steering in an isolated ship, through a stable environment, to a destination. In a sailboat race, a chain of command still exists. But the captain is constantly monitoring the environment, being highly sensitive and often responding tactically and strategically to shifts in competitors' behavior, team and boat capabilities, wind conditions, and water current. (Kaplan and Norton, 1996, p. 16)

This is a far cry from the stick figure-like metaphors of the traditional economic and accounting models, and it is far more accurate and helpful.

To summarize this discussion, the balanced scorecard, with its inclusion of multiple measures of performance, helps wean managers away from myopic, bottom-line thinking. Where the traditional measure of corporate performance—net income—creates the impression that there exists a single magical number, the balanced scorecard lays out the case for a more subtle and realistic approach. Consider, for example, the company in their sample that undertook safety audits across all operational areas, tracked customer loyalty and employee satisfaction, and set key targets from an internal environmental audit program as part of the balanced scorecard approach (see p. 205).

Further, the balanced scorecard will lead managers on a search for missing measures. A more reasonable approach to measuring corporate activities will almost necessarily convince managers that they may know what to measure (e.g., corporate reputation and image; see p. 75) but not necessarily how to measure it. Such a realization may spur them on to develop those measures.

In addition to developing new measures, the balanced scorecard may even convince managers that words also convey meaning. More managers will begin to emulate Warren Buffett and incorporate substantive text where numbers alone cannot convey the whole message (see Kaplan and Norton 1996, p. 145).

Finally, every corporation has a story. The balanced scorecard helps managers to tell the story in a credible way to corporate stakeholders. It should be created with the input of employees at all levels of the organization and be made available to them, it should help the corporate board fulfill its oversight role by becoming the focus of corporate board meetings, and it should ultimately allow investors and potential investors to better track investment opportunities. As Kaplan and Norton explicitly state, "The best financial reporting policies will eventually be derived from the best internal reporting policies" (p. 210).

To be sure, the balanced scorecard, as conceived by Kaplan and Norton, is a purely commodity-based approach (one might even be tempted to call it "stakeholder accounting"). The ambiguity that Kaplan and Norton embrace is a "constrained" ambiguity about the best means for achieving shareholder goals. That shareholders care only about the maximization of profits is not an ambiguous proposition. The authors consistently justify the balanced scorecard in traditional financial terms. Nevertheless (and in spite of the authors' own qualifications), the balanced scorecard is a positive development toward building useful and pragmatic measures of corporate activities—a foundation of legitimate transparency.

Warren Bennis and Patricia Ward Biederman in their book *Organizing Genius: The Secrets of Creative Collaboration* have noted what great leaders have always known:

They know that we long for meaning. Without meaning, labor is time stolen from us. We become like Milton's fallen Samson, "a slave at the wheel." . . . Problem solving is the task we evolved for. It gives us as much pleasure as sex does. Leaders of Great Groups grasp this intuitively. They know that work done for its own sake becomes a wonderful game. (1997, p. 23)

At one point, Kaplan and Norton summarize: "Ultimately the ability to meet ambitious targets for financial, customer, and internal-business-process objectives depends on organizational capabilities for learning and growth" (p. 146). In light of Bennis and Biederman's observation, I would only add, at the end of the day, learning and growth will depend on the quest for human meaning.

8

Do Meaning-Based Organizations Really Exist?

By this point, one might be convinced that the idea of a meaning-based organization is intriguing and idealistic but wholly impractical. In other words, it sounds good on paper, but will it fly? In fact, this final chapter suggests, to the contrary, that meaning-based organizations are ubiquitous. Who says "organization" says "meaning," amending a famous organizational rule by the German sociologist Robert Michels (1962). It is not that some organizations are meaning-based, and others are not. Rather, some organizations are self-consciously meaning-based, and others are less so. Meaning is like air; if human beings are to survive as human beings, meaning must be everywhere.

Managers and other key employees who insist that the organization is simply a utilitarian tool and that "business is business" are either misguided, lying, or both. For better or for worse, business is also a location where human beings constantly and forever interpret life's meanings. This statement, in and of itself, is not meant to be an ethical statement necessarily implying specific actions of any particular sort. By itself, it is no more prescriptive than the sentence, "The boy is six feet tall." It stands or falls as a purely descriptive observation. It is verifiable (or not) through surveys, observations, content analysis, interviews, self-reflection, and other sociological techniques. But, if it is true, as I believe the overwhelming preponderance of evidence suggests, it implies a number of very specific managerial corollaries. The remainder of this chapter explores three of these implications.

GOAL SEEKING AND NOTHING ELSE: AN IMPOSSIBLE NIGHTMARE

First of all, if organizations provide locations where human beings interpret life, it implies the following: *it is impossible to design and construct a fully functioning, commodity-based organization.* Purely instrumental organizations, goal seeking and nothing else, cannot exist. Even if this is how an organization was initially conceived and designed, in practice, managers and other stakeholders immediately get back to the hard work of interpretation. An organization designed to operate like a machine and only like a machine would almost certainly alter the kinds of interpretations that corporate players choose. It would produce a perverse and ultimately inhuman kind of meaning in the organization, but meaning, nonetheless. Businesses are zones of meaning, whether we like it or not.

Almost 30 years ago John Ladd, writing in *The Monist,* suggested the following:

Actions that are wrong by ordinary standards are not so for organizations; indeed, they may often be required. Secrecy, espionage, and deception do not make organizational action wrong; rather, they are right, proper and, indeed, *rational,* if they serve the objectives of the organization. They are no more or less wrong than, say, bluffing is in poker. From the point of view of organizational decision-making they are "ethically neutral." . . . Organizations are like machines, and it would be a category mistake to expect a machine to comply with the principles of morality. By the same token, an official or agent of a formal organization is simply violating the basic rule of organizational activity if he allows his moral scruples rather than the objectives of the organization to determine his decision. (1970, p. 499; emphasis added)

Inherent in Ladd's position—the ethical correctness of an action is to be judged solely in terms of its links to organization goals—is a kind of meaning that doesn't want to know about itself. Ladd is like a magician who merely says, "I'm invisible" and then thinks that he really is. It is true that, in some ways, organizations are like machines, but in other crucial ways they are not. Most fundamentally, organizations—unlike machines—are always composed of individual human beings. Regardless of how tightly roles are defined in the organization, it is always a human being, engaged in the process of interpretation, who is playing at the role.

Contrary to Ladd, I very much doubt that any real-world manager has ever sat down and actually tried to design a purely commodity-based enterprise, attempting, once and for all, to purge the organization of any and all traces of humanity. One can only imagine the final results, but three predictions are obvious. First, the organization and its human actors would begin to engage in activities that most of us would probably consider far from "ethically neutral." If management somehow successfully created an organization in which the corporate culture supported any and all activities undertaken under the banner of promoting corporate goals, it is quite likely that such an atmosphere would encourage workers to cut corners, lie, misuse corporate assets, and cheat customers. Employees would begin to reason that if the organization lives outside the ethical world, perhaps they (especially in their role as managers) do, as well. Second, the experiences of working in such an environment would dramatically alter and change managers and employees in fundamental ways. It would be virtually impossible for employees to live 40 hours per week or more in a so-called ethically neutral environment and not have this alter their character. Third, Ladd's machine-like environment would ultimately self-destruct. Some of these organizations might last longer than others, but in the end all of them would topple under their own weight. Discussions about meaning, purpose, responsibility, and significance, far from being shut out of organizational life, would multiply and expand to the point that they would ultimately tear open the "iron cage" of the purely commodity-based organization.

Good managers intuitively know all of this, and so do our best writers. In the movie *Glengarry GlenRoss*, written by David Mamet and based on his Pulitzer Prize-winning play, the viewer is introduced to a real estate firm known as Premiere Properties. The movie examines the professional lives of four salesmen and one sales manager (all men) as they slowly and laboriously attempt to survive 24 more hours on the job in a drab office situated in an unidentified urban environment.

Premiere Properties, I certainly hope, is as close as one will ever come to a purely commodity-based organization. At a meeting that sets the tone for the remainder of the day, an unnamed man from "downtown," representing the absentee owners, Mitch and Murray, reminds the salesmen that the only thing that really counts is getting the customer to sign on the dotted line. The organization's motto is the often-repeated mantra:

ABC—always be closing. As the anonymous representative puts it, "You close or you hit the bricks. . . . Are you man enough to take it?"

To underscore the seriousness of his macho message, the man from downtown reveals the company's new employee incentive package. Top salesman for the month wins a Cadillac Eldorado, second-place finisher gets a set of steak knives, and everyone else gets fired. A large blackboard with each of the salesmen's names is used to keep track of performance to date and to remind employees that to Mitch and Murray they are nothing but a single number. In one column it lists the salesmen's names, and in another column it shows the total dollar amount of revenue brought in by them during the month. The blackboard sits in the middle of the office. Nothing else could, because nothing else matters. As the man from downtown makes his exit in his self-described $85,000 BMW, one of the salesmen asks him his name. Without missing a beat he coldly responds, "You see this watch. This watch costs more than your car. . . . That's who I am."

The office manager, John Williamson (he has a name but not much of a character), reinforces the Mitch and Murray strategy, doling out two leads per day to the salesmen (no more and no less) and justifies his stingy and impersonal attitude to everyone, including himself, by muttering, "I don't make the rules" or, just a few moments later, "I do what I'm hired to do . . . what I'm told."

Not unexpectedly, given this environment, salesmen lie freely to customers, inventing fictitious secretaries and competing customers to impress and intimidate outsiders, giving themselves undeserved promotions, and changing crucial dates to suit their own interests.

Even when they aren't lying, they begin to talk as if they are. At Premiere Properties, lying becomes a good in and of itself. In fact, the cardinal rule at the company is not the more conventional "Thou shalt not lie" but "When you do lie, make sure it helps the company," as Shelley "the machine" Levene puts it. As odd at this "principle" sounds, it follows directly, of course, from a full embrace of the commodity-based perspective. Ladd would have to call this behavior "ethically neutral"; I'm not sure anyone else would.

As the story unfolds, the weather outside intensifies, and the background thunder is suddenly in the foreground. Two of the salesmen begin to hatch a plan to steal the much-desired (among the salesmen) Glengarry leads from the office. They can be sold for $7,500 to a competing firm. "What can you do if you don't have the leads?" they rhetorically ask each other. They further justify the planned theft by claiming, "Somebody should do something to them [Mitch and Murray] to hurt them where they live." These salesmen were otherwise law-abiding citizens. Their experiences in the organization have fundamentally altered them to the point where they can contemplate, justify, and carry out a serious crime.

Mitch and Murray's attempt to get the salesmen to recognize that the only thing that counts is the bottom line is doomed to failure from the start. One cannot prevent people from interpreting life's meanings simply by telling them to stop or even paying them to cease. These employees are as much philosophers and storytellers as they are salesmen. The star salesman, Ricky Roma, is overheard talking to a potential customer, "Our life is looking forward or back, where's the moment?" Later in the same conversation Roma points out, "You try to stave off insecurity, but you can't." As another salesman, Dave Moss, puts it right before the theft, "We're men here. I'll tell you what the hard part is. It is standing up." As the plotters come to understand it, stealing the good Glengarry leads is an act of liberation that will set them free, once and for all. The salesmen are in it for the money, for sure. But more importantly, they begin to interpret the planned theft as an act of courage and heroism. It is something that they must do to maintain their dignity and their sense of self-worth. Amazingly enough, in the context of David Mamet's Premiere Properties this is something very difficult for a viewer to find fault with. As it turns out, not surprisingly, Shelley "the machine" Levene is no machine at all.

Life in the organization, according to Mamet's vision, is as much about the quest for meaning as anything else. In the end, the office is trashed, friendships unravel, lives are forever ruined, and the thieves are caught. Premiere Properties will hobble along for a while, even if it needs to hire replacement salesmen. But I doubt that any savvy investor would consider putting his or her money into this enterprise as a long-term investment. *Glengarry GlenRoss* might plausibly be seen as an indictment against business, all business, as my business students often argue. I think this misses the point, however. The story does not necessarily suggest a broad attack on capitalism, but the real lesson of Mamet's thought experiment is a more modest, but more important, one. It is impossible to design and construct a fully functioning, commodity-based organization. Purely instrumental organizations, goal seeking and nothing else, cannot exist. Claiming that you are removing meaning as a corporate strategy does not actually imply that it has been removed. Philip Selznick, in his thought-provoking book *The Moral Commonwealth*, put the same point, more formally, as follows: "An organization that *tries* to be instrumentally single-minded, guided wholly by norms of purposive rationality, nonetheless finds itself faced with more comprehensive obligations" (Selznick, 1992, p. 291). This is true because as organizations become institutionalized, they become infused with value "beyond the technical requirements of the task at hand" (Selznick, 1984, p. 17). As long as humans continue to populate organizations, meaning is here to stay.

MORE IS BETTER

If it is impossible to purge the organization of meaning, a second managerial corollary follows: *all things being equal, the more self-conscious stakeholders become about organizational meanings, the better.* This is true for all organizations, but especially true for those that myopically focus on bottom-line concerns to the neglect of everything else. Every company has a story, and every company's story provides a key with which to unlock organizational meanings. Managers are not like lions fighting over a fresh carcass but are more often like rabbinic sages arguing over the true significance of an obscure Talmudic passage.

Consider the case of ServiceMaster, a Chicago-based, outsourcing services company employing more than 200,000 people and serving more than 6 million customers in 30 countries across the world. The company earned revenues of more than $4 billion in 1997 and was ranked 373 in the Fortune 500 list. Visit the Web site at www.svm.com and click on "Our Story." You will read about Marion E. Wade, the former minor league baseball player turned entrepreneur. In 1929, working out of his home, Wade started a mothproofing company, and it was from this small mothproofing company that ServiceMaster grew. How so? Read on:

Marion Wade had a strong personal faith and a desire to honor God in all he did. Translating this into the market place, he viewed each individual employee and customer as being made in God's image—worthy of dignity and respect. This view also was shared by his successors, Ken Hansen—with his financial prowess and ever present bow tie—and Ken Wessner, a superb operating person with a desire to develop people. These three shaped what became our company objectives: To honor God in all we do; To help people develop; To pursue excellence; and To grow profitably.

To the managers at ServiceMaster these goals are so important and pervasive that they literally had them chiseled in marble on the walls of the lobby of corporate headquarters. In C. William Pollard's words, "The marble wall conveys a permanency that does not change. The principles carved in this stone are lasting" (1996, p. 19). Even someone solely interested in financial returns might want to take notice of this story. ServiceMaster has been one of the top performers in the U.S. economy over the past ten years. Investors in ServiceMaster have earned an annualized average return of 33 percent, even outperforming such a high-flier as Coca-Cola.

A more self-conscious attitude toward meaning (and the interpretation of meaning) on the part of corporate stakeholders will improve organizations in several distinct and practical ways. To a large extent, that is what this book has attempted to demonstrate. One of the main points of Chapter 3, for example, was that stakeholders imbued with a meaning-based perspective will be more likely to search out and discover alternative decision-making procedures that will ultimately lead to better decision outcomes. Chapter 4 argued that a meaning-based perspective will yield a fuller and more accurate understanding of fairness in the organization. Fairness is not always something imposed by outsiders but is also understood as an internal requirement.

The most important point to emphasize here is that the meaning-based perspective is better because it provides a better understanding of what organizations are really like. The idea of the meaning-based organization takes the flat, two-dimensional view of the economists and adds an entirely new dimension to our thinking.

In more practical terms, this perspective helps to clarify many of the most important corporate actions. As Thomas Peters reminds us, "Symbols are the very stuff of management behavior. Executives, after all, do not synthesize chemicals or operate lift trucks; they deal in symbols" (1978, p. 10). Managers who become more self-conscious about organizational meanings will have a better and more nuanced understanding of organizational restructuring, executive succession, the use of physical space, employee compensation, and many other issues. The meaning-based perspective is also a pragmatic one.

Organizational Restructuring

No doubt managers restructure organizations for a variety of reasons, including purely efficiency considerations. Nevertheless, every restructuring necessarily alters corporate meanings, as well. The success or failure of any restructuring hinges on how well meaning is understood and managed, not only on how well emerging roles are specified. Jeffrey Pfeffer notes, "A restructuring which creates a new product-development department, a consumer affairs department, or a public relations department provides a visible manifestation to those inside and outside of the organization that the activity presumably within the purview of the newly created department has become more important to the organization" (Pfeffer, 1981, p. 39). Restructuring is thus understood as an attempt to tell a new corporate story. Armed with this insight, perhaps managers will be able to tell better and more convincing stories.

Executive Succession

Often managers are fired, even though no one could have possibly foreseen or controlled the negative events that ultimately led to their undoing. This is easiest to see in the case of sports teams but occurs in other businesses as well. Organizations, especially in desperate situations, often want to start over. Replacing the current chief executive officer is a symbolic attempt to say, "That chapter is over!" Similarly, hiring a new manager provides an organization with a way of tapping into some other organization's narrative. For example, when the New York Jets hired Bill Parcells, no doubt the team hired him for his technical knowledge and expertise of the game, but the organization also hired him in an attempt to "purchase" the New England Patriots' success story. The Jets front office desperately needed to create a new culture and reasoned (perhaps correctly) that a new and powerful coach with an outstanding track record was a necessary first step.

Physical Space

The design of an office building conveys meaning. Is it the biggest building in town? Is it the most modern? Is a particular department centrally located? Whose office has the best view? Do employees work in open spaces or closed spaces? The answers to all of these questions reveal deep-seated corporate philosophies and may help organizational leaders better understand and manage the organization.

Compensation

Salary levels are important because they directly affect employees' living standards. They are also important because they convey information about the pecking order in an organization. (Who's on top? Who's not?) Even a small difference in salary can have huge impacts in terms of corporate interpretations. It is extremely difficult for underpaid managers to get others to respect them and to get things done.

Not only is the amount of compensation an important piece of information, but the method of compensation is also telling. Stock option plans are often defended purely in terms of motivation. It is argued that employees will work harder and more efficiently if their compensation is directly linked to stock price performance. Less often appreciated is the symbolic importance of such programs. Implementing an employee stock option program sends a strong and unambiguous message to stakeholders that stock price performance is now the new measuring rod.

Other corporate actions, such as the choice of a corporate name (what will the name of a newly merged company convey?), the selection of a logo, the development of a theme for an annual report (how many pictures of women and minorities will the final report include?), the choice of a particular consulting or auditing firm, and even the purchase of a new computer system, are all meaning-events and are understood as such (or at least should be) by corporate stakeholders, as much as anything else they might be. If it is self-evident that corporate leaders need a managerial theory that corresponds well to reality, it is just as self-evident that the more that managers and others become aware of corporate meanings and how to manage them, the better. Even the simplest corporate actions will provoke stakeholders into yet another round of interpretations. Perhaps the real question is not whether or not meaning-based organizations exist, but how did we ever come to believe that they might not?

Martin Rosenblum, an employee of Harley-Davidson, was quoted recently in *Fortune* magazine (Dumaine, 1994). He was asked what ultimately motivated him. His answer is worth quoting and considering:

The reason I get up very early and get down to the Harley-Davidson office immediately is that the company has soul. There really is a mystique involved with this motorcycle company that is rightly labeled its soul. I can't define it, but I know it's there.

Let me try to explain it. I've never been a joiner. In the fifties, when I raced hot rods, instead of a club plaque on my rear fender, mine said LONE WOLF, NO CLUB. Before I came to Harley, I was in the music business, and I wrote poetry. I also taught English for ten years at the University of Wisconsin. But at Harley it's different. For the first time in my life I've encountered a lifelong learning process that says that leadership involves not a dynamic personality, not a command-and-control mentality, but the ability to empower others as well as yourself. Yes I've got tattoos. Yes, I'm a hard-core rider. But what I'm talking about goes beyond just getting a job done. It is about a very complex, difficult, personal transformation.

Harley's CEO, Richard Teerlink, spends much of his time self-consciously trying to create an environment conducive to meaningful work, an environment that will be both financially rewarding and compelling to employees like Martin Rosenblum. Ultimately, the real goal of business ethics is not to add more rules (thou shalt not do this, thou shalt not do that) but to help managers become more aware of just how important business really is. For many, like Martin Rosenblum, it is why they get up in the morning.

ALL MEANINGS ARE NOT CREATED EQUAL

The more self-conscious that corporate participants are about the meaning-based perspective, the more they will come to recognize the third and final managerial corollary: *all meanings are not morally equivalent*. Simply put, some interpretations are better than others, but distinguishing among them is not always easy. The meaning-based perspective is not a panacea. As Selznick (1992) put it, "From a moral point of view, institutionalization may be positive or negative. Much depends on *what* is institutionalized" (p. 234). Warren Bennis and Patricia Ward Biederman (1997) call this the "Wannsee question."

Wannsee, of course, was the suburb of Berlin where Hitler's minions gathered in 1942 and formulated the plan for the murder of the world's Jews. The question: Can creative collaboration take place in an evil cause? The answer is yes. The men at Wannsee were no geniuses, but, united by a single, evil vision, using cutting-edge technology and working with missionary zeal, they nearly destroyed an entire people in just three years. . . . Whether you are part of a group that is developing a cure for cancer or one that is creating a weapon that could destroy the human race, the intense pleasures of creative collaboration can cause a kind of moral paralysis. (p. 217)

In other words, embracing a meaning-based perspective, as the preceding example amply demonstrates, is not the end of business ethics but the *beginning* of a new way of doing business ethics. Unabashedly introducing values is not a revolutionary call; it merely asks us to recognize and reflect on what we're already doing. "We do not discover the moral world because we have always lived there. We do not have to invent it because it has already been invented. . . . Moral argument in such a setting is interpretive in character, closely resembling the work of a lawyer or judge who struggles to find meaning in a morass of conflicting laws and precedents" (Walzer, 1987, p. 20).

This book is a call for organizational ethics, but a new kind of self-aware organizational ethics built upon a better and more accurate definition of the organization. At the individual, corporate, national, and global levels we have to come to learn what is really worth seeking from life, and we have to learn to develop peaceful, just, and fair ways of resolving the conflicts that inevitably arise.

As stakeholders become more sophisticated about the centrality of corporate meanings, they are realizing that many of the struggles encountered in the organizational setting are contests of meaning more than old-fashioned contests of power. Disagreements are less often about who gets what and more often about whose interpretations will win the day. Too often sophisticated analysts recognize the importance of all of this but then feel compelled to point out that they (the sophisticated analysts) understand that this search for meaning is really irrational. In answering the question of why symbolic action is possible, for example, Pfeffer suggests "that it must be the case that at least some substantial portion of persons interested in the organization . . . must be unable to discern with any certainty whether or what they are obtaining from the organization. *In other words, symbolic outcomes will suffice if those in contact with the organization are unable to discriminate reality from symbol* (Pfeffer, 1981, p. 28; emphasis added). Pfeffer and others (e.g., see Edelman, 1964) never even seriously contemplate the possibility that our attachment to symbols and the quest for human meaning create the very foundations of "reality" and constitute the most sophisticated game in town.

This book suggests that business ethics will be improved to the extent that the meaning-based perspective takes center stage. Managers and other corporate stakeholders are beginning to ask and answer each of the seven questions posed and discussed earlier. As we begin to ask, What is business ethics, and how do ethical decisions happen?, it dawns on the sensitive manager that there is more to life, including organizational life, than the draconian pursuit of self-interest to the neglect of everything else. We begin to wonder whether or not it's possible to define fairness. Is fairness merely an external constraint imposed upon us by competitors, or is fairness something that should be woven into the very fabric of organizational structures? But even with an enlarged understanding of fairness, is fairness, by itself, sufficient? Can organizations help to satisfy our highest-level human needs? As we enter into the knowledge-based economy—and beyond—are organizations necessary for self-actualization? Can religion play a helpful role here? We begin to realize that even with preliminary answers to these questions, we still need outstanding managers and strong leadership. How does one even begin to measure business ethics and lead in the meaning-based organization?

The purpose of this book has not been to offer definitive answers to these questions but to help "jump-start" business ethics conversations. If the earlier questions are worthy of our energy, attention, and focus, and if organizations and their members are beginning to develop preliminary answers, then meaning-based organizations already exist!

YOUR MEANING, MY MEANING, AND OUR MEANING: THE FUTURE OF BUSINESS ETHICS

As managers continue this "process of business ethics" in the future, new questions (and hopefully new answers) will begin to emerge. The ultimate success or failure of the business ethics movement will hinge on whether or not we can meet the following significant challenges summarized in the form of three additional, future-oriented questions.

The Question of Language

Is there a language that we can further develop to allow organizations to openly discuss and judge the value of alternative meanings? To a large extent, business ethics is a kind of language. Many of the advances in business ethics over the last 25 years or so can be thought of as an attempt to broaden and institutionalize its vocabulary and syntax. Some of the gains here have been quite impressive.

A significant number of major corporations have endorsed the ten social responsibility principles authored by the Coalition for Environmentally Responsible Economics (CERES). In addition, many corporations have written cogent and compelling codes of conduct. As just one example, Rubbermaid, Inc. articulates the following message:

We believe that internal partnerships, *meaningful teamwork*, and ongoing learning will instill in every Rubbermaid associate the skills, the understanding, and the desire to achieve continuous improvement in every link of our value chain. (emphasis added)

The document continues with an emphasis on the corporation's commitment to "mutual respect," "integrity and ethical conduct," "safety and protection of the environment," and "fair return on investment."

Many major corporations now have ethics officers and various types of ethics program in place. There is even an Ethics Officer Association, inaugurated in the summer of 1991, which is "dedicated to promoting ethical business practices and serving as a forum for the exchange of information and strategies among individual responsible for ethics programs" (Hoffman, 1995, p. 399). In 1992, a new organization called Business for Social Responsibility was formed. Today it is a national association with more than 800 members and affiliates, including AT&T, Federal Express, Hallmark, Hasbro, Levi Strauss, Polaroid, Reebok, Starbucks, and Time Warner, to name just a few.

Further, many companies have begun to implement ethics audits, and some of the major accounting firms now have partners in charge of ethics-related issues. Many investors, including some of the largest institutional investors, have adopted the notion of social responsibility investing, and there now exist numerous mutual funds to promote this goal. There are many conferences for both businesspeople and academics on business ethics across North America and the world. The First World Congress of Business, Economics, and Ethics was convened in Tokyo, Japan, in July 1996. Among some of the items discussed there were the Caux Round Table Principles. These international business ethics principles are rooted in two basic ideals, the Japanese principle of *kyosei* (which roughly means living and working together for the common good) and human dignity. There are academic journals and popular magazines devoted specifically to business ethics, including the *Journal of Business Ethics, Business Ethics Quarterly*, and *Research on Accounting Ethics*.

Unfortunately, even with such solid and seemingly permanent gains in place, one still senses that business ethics is not something that can be openly discussed at business meetings without first apologizing. Barbara Ley Toffler's disturbing summary of the business climate, based on hundreds of interviews with business executives, is still just as true today as it was when she first wrote it. "Although more and more companies are stating publicly their own commitment to ethics in management, few individuals find it comfortable to raise such concerns (unless they can couch those concerns in other words). There seems to be a sense among managers that talking about ethics is 'just not done here.' And, unfortunately they are usually right'' (Toffler, 1986, p. 337). Corporate codes are written off as mere public relations; ethics officers and corporate ethics programs are in place to head off costly litigation and have little to do with the truly meaning-based organization; and conferences, journals, and magazines are all talk and no action, or, at least, this is how the challenges are framed.

Business ethics is not yet integral to business. Even against the impressive background of tangible gains outlined earlier, there continues to be an advantage to the cynics who "talk the talk" but don't yet "walk the walk." This is a problem for the cynics, but it is our problem as well. I suggest that the reason business ethics is still not fully integrated with business results from the continued focus on a rule-based or recipe approach to business ethics. The grammar of business ethics is not yet perfected. Its development in the coming years should be undertaken with an eye toward pluralism and toleration. Is there a way to "agree to disagree" when we are arguing about meanings (and not widgets) and still maintain one's integrity? Can we learn to live and thrive in organizations that openly recognize and honor *your* meaning and *my* meaning, while all the while trying to self-consciously understand and promote *our* meaning? Above all, we need to avoid a Big Brother mentality in which corporations begin to dictate how we feel and how we think.

Do the Stories Have Anything to Do with Reality?

As corporate stories are taken more seriously, and as business ethics is understood as a language (as opposed to a set of simple rules), a second, related question emerges: Does the written version of the corporate story correspond to the oral version (the story in use)?

The Jewish tradition distinguishes between the written law (the Bible) and the oral law (the numerous commentaries and codes based on the Bible). The written law is considered to be fixed and never-changing, while the oral law is open and constantly evolving to meet the needs of contemporary communities. There is a tension created when one openly acknowledges the existence of two versions of the same story. Nevertheless, my instinct is that most mature ethical communities recognize the distinction between aspirations and realities. That is who I want to be, and this is who I am.

Companies like Ben and Jerry's, the Body Shop, Tom's of Maine, Stonyfield Farm Yogurt, Working Assets Funding Service, ServiceMaster, Herman Miller, Hewlett-Packard, Johnson & Johnson, Nordstrom's, and a growing list of other transparently meaning-based organizations (large and small) open themselves up to a new kind of attack. The attack centers on the allegation of hypocrisy—professing a set of beliefs that one does not really possess. Each of these companies has a clearly expressed vision and an explicit and carefully thought out set of corporate values that infuse the organization and are well publicized. In each case top management stands tall behind the message. Given such prominence to ethics and values, there is clearly a new type of risk associated with the meaning-based organization. What happens when the written version of the story does not correspond to the oral one?

While it might be considered silly to question whether or not Haagen-Dazs should be promoting a high-fat frozen dessert product, it becomes a fair and even urgent question when posed to a Ben and Jerry's. After all, if Ben Cohen and Jerry Greenfield are worried about the rain forest, shouldn't they also concern themselves with domestic health problems? Obesity and high cholesterol are directly linked to heart attacks and other heart-related diseases. If the consumption of high-fat products leads to high cholesterol, as most of the current medical evidence suggests, one wonders how long a socially responsive and "values-led business" can ignore this question. I do not doubt the integrity and professed idealism of Ben and Jerry. Their new book, *Ben & Jerry's Double-Dip: How to Run a Values-Led Business and Make Money, Too* (1997), is an absolute must-read for anyone interested in implementing the ideas discussed in this book. Both the company and the book constitute core pieces of evidence that business ethics works, even in the real world. Nevertheless, one should read and evaluate its message carefully and with a healthy dose of skepticism.

The Body Shop has also come under intense media scrutiny. In an article published in the September/October 1994 issue of *Business Ethics*, Jon Entine challenged many of the social responsibility claims of the company. Arguing that the company's reputation has been based more on image than reality, Entine cataloged a number of complaints:

- Products described as "natural" contained petrochemicals and preservatives.

- The use of products with exotic origins was fabricated.

- Third World sourcing of ingredients was exaggerated.

- Environmental practices fell far short of company statements.

- Charitable contributions fell far short of company statements.
- Franchisee relations were under Federal Trade Commission (FTC) investigation.

Gordon Roddick, the chairman of the Body Shop, responded in an open letter that also appeared in the same magazine. In a point-by-point rebuttal, Roddick questions the integrity of Entine's sources and the accuracy of his claims. When one carefully examines this controversy, one notices that it is essentially a question about either integrity or hypocrisy. Whether or not Entine's critiques are true, they are interesting and important only because of the prior claims of the Body Shop. If the Body Shop was not self-consciously trying to promote meaning, Entine's critique would lose much of its force.

In its mission statement the Body Shop explicitly lists its reasons for being:

To Dedicate our business to the pursuit of social and environmental change.

To Creatively balance the financial and human needs of our stakeholders: employees, customers, franchisees, suppliers and shareholders. . . .

To Meaningfully contribute to local, national and international communities in which we trade, by a adopting a code of conduct which ensures care, honesty, fairness and respect. . . .

To Tirelessly work to narrow the gap between principle and practice, whilst making fun, passion and care part of our daily lives.

My point in all of this is not to take sides between Entine and the Body Shop. Rather, I cite this material as evidence of the increasing seriousness and gravity of the business ethics debate and movement. Companies like Ben & Jerry's and the Body Shop are more vulnerable than traditional (and less articulate) companies to certain kinds of external attack. This is to be expected, as it comes with the territory.

In summing up this section, there are lessons for everyone here. Advocates of the meaning-based organization should never overstate their case. After all, Ben & Jerry's is still an ice cream company, and the Body Shop still sells cosmetics. Consumers and other interested parties should recognize that there will always be a distinction between ideals and actions; the written and oral versions are never perfectly consistent. Finally, critics should clarify what they are against. I'm afraid that much of the criticism against Ben & Jerry's, the Body Shop, and other leading values-led companies is not motivated out of a love of business ethics but is there to show us that business ethics itself is impossible. Why else pick on these companies? Aren't there bigger fish to fry?

Where Do You Draw the Line? (Or Do You Draw the Line?)

I believe that the single most important topic that will dominate discussions about business and business ethics in the future will focus on the deep and seemingly impenetrable problem about how to understand the relationship between the meaning-based and the commodity-based perspectives. A major theme of this book has been that the traditional answers to this question are no longer tenable.

Economists, for the most part, continue to argue that the concept of meaning is itself meaningless. They assert, mainly through their silence on this question, that there is no real problem concerning the relationship between the meaning-based and commodity-based perspectives because there is only one plausible view, the commodity-based perspective. Economists advocate translating everything into rationalistic terms that don't allow for discussions about human purposes, growth, self-actualization, and transformation. What they cannot admit is that this approach itself entails an "ought" (decisions *ought* to be framed in rationalistic terms) and therefore requires some minimal moral argument and backing. Some economists, of course, have recognized this paradox and attempt to derive a kind of thin moral vocabulary from the discipline's own rationalistic foundations.

Many thinkers, more at home in the humanities, take almost the exact opposite tack here. Like the economists, they see no real difficulty or interesting intellectual challenge in understanding the relationship between the meaning-based and the commodity-based perspectives. For these thinkers, it's not that the meaning-based perspective is meaningless (as the economists believe) but that the commodity-based perspective is meaningless. Some of my best friends in the humanities seem to take a perverse delight in demonstrating their complete ignorance on matters of economics and business. They boast of not reading the business section of the *New York Times* (as if this was a badge of courage) and mock those who read the *Wall Street Journal* as uncultured and lacking in true sophistication. Alan Bloom's unduly harsh critique of business schools—"the effect of the MBA is to corral a horde of students who want to get into business school and put the *blinders on them*" (Bloom, 1987, p. 371;

emphasis added)—ultimately derives its power from the undefended assertion that the commodity-based perspective is completely incoherent.

I think for most of us, however, neither of these two extreme positions is a viable option. On one hand, it is self-evidently true that talk of meaning is not mere rhetoric but is the essential human activity. On the other hand, it is equally clear that the commodity-based perspective is one of the great human inventions. In many ways, the commodity-based perspective is like the goose that lays the golden eggs. It is no mere coincidence that the commodity-based perspective emerged at the dawn of the Industrial Revolution and that its clearest articulation by Adam Smith immediately preceded the greatest increase in material benefits that the world has ever seen. When Milton Friedman (1962) observes that today a good fraction of the world's population eats like the kings of the past, it is no exaggeration. We live longer than ever before, we wear better-quality clothes, we travel farther, we can communicate with each other more easily and at much lower costs, we have access to better health care, we allocate risk more efficiently, and we are better prepared to meet all kinds of personal and natural catastrophes. In material terms, there can be little debate that most humans are better off today than their ancestors were 500 years ago. I think it is just as clear that such great advances are, in large part, due to the fact humans have become more rational, not less, and have learned to organize themselves more efficiently, not less. Defining organizations as utilitarian tools designed to satisfy preexisting wants and preferences, as the commodity-based perspective does, has been an insight that has paid enormous material dividends.

For the majority who view both the meaning-based and commodity-based perspectives as real, there continue to exist two interpretive possibilities. Possibility 1: both perspectives are real, yet there is no inherent conflict between them because each perspective deals with a different realm of existence. It is as if the meaning-based perspective and the commodity-based perspective belong in two hermetically sealed jars—and the contents of one never intermingle with the contents of the other. There are for-profit organizations and not-for-profit organizations. There are the public realm and the private realm, the holy and the profane, work and play.

In many ways, John D. Rockefeller is the icon and one of the greatest authors of this dual-world theory. Ron Chernow concludes his recent biography of Rockefeller with the following paradoxical description. First, Chernow describes Rockefeller as businessman:

Starting in the 1870s, Rockefeller's stewardship of Standard Oil had signalled a new era in American life that had both inspired and alarmed the populace. His unequaled brilliance and rapacity as a businessman had squarely confronted the country with troubling questions about the shape of the economy, the distribution of wealth, and the proper relationship between business and government. . . . In creating new corporate forms, he charted the way for the modern multinational corporations that came to dominate economic life in the twentieth century. But in so doing he also exposed the manifold abuses that could accompany untrammeled economic power, especially in the threat to elected government.

Second, Chernow characterizes Rockefeller as charitable man:

The fiercest robber baron had turned out to be the foremost philanthropist. . . . He established the promotion of knowledge, especially scientific knowledge, as a task no less important than giving alms to the poor or building schools, hospitals, and museums. . . . By the time Rockefeller died, in fact, so much good had unexpectedly flowered from so much evil that God might even have greeted him on the other side, as the titan had so confidently expected all along. (1998, p. 676)

Whether or not God actually greeted Rockefeller upon his demise as Chernow suggests he might have, Rockefeller's life demonstrates the viability (if not the attraction) of the dual-world theory. If managers, stockholders, employees, and consumers complain that they feel as if they live in two worlds, it's because they really do.

Possibility 2: both the meaning-based and the commodity-based perspectives are real, both perspectives deal with the same reality (there is only one world, not two), and, in fact, both perspectives (to a point) reinforce one another. The meaning-based and commodity-based perspectives are not at war with one another, although it may often seem that they are. There is no zero-sum relationship where more of one necessarily means less of the other. The meaning-based perspective and the commodity-based perspective depend on each other. This second possibility is the interpretive stance adopted and advocated here.

Amitai Etzioni, in his 1995 presidential address to the American Sociological Association (and in his book based on the paper, *The New Golden Rule*, 1996a), described the relationship between centripetal and centrifugal communal forces. He noted that all social entities are subject to both forces. Centripetal forces "seek to pull in members' commitments, energies, time, and resources for what the community as a collectivity endorses as its notion of the common good. . . . They oppose excessive withdrawal into self and self-centered projects, but do not oppose individual endeavors that might be compatible with, or contribute to, the common good" (1996a, p. 6). At the same time, the quest for autonomy generates "centrifugal forces, forces that, if they reach high levels, undermine the communal bonds and culture" (1996a, p. 6). These inward- and outward-pulling forces vie with one another continually. The tug-of-war between them is not accidental but influences all communities, including the business organization. Etzioni believes that the typical relationship between these two kinds of forces (up to a point) is symbiotic in nature; the two forces enrich and strengthen one another rather than cancel each other out. Etzioni compares the relationship between centripetal and centrifugal forces to the relationship between plover birds and crocodiles. Plover birds courageously stand in the mouths of crocodiles, eating worms and leeches. In such a way, the plover birds enjoy a rich and nutritious diet, while the crocodiles get their teeth cleaned.

The relationship between the meaning-based (centripetal) and commodity-based (centrifugal) perspectives can also be understood as symbiotic in nature. The commodity-based perspective (with all of its many benefits duly noted earlier) grows out of the fertile and nutrient-rich soil of the meaning-based perspective. Just as freedom requires order, the rational model of decision making requires the model of appropriateness. At the same time, however, the meaning-based perspective thrives and matures only to the extent that the organization can afford such luxuries. More material wealth and more rationality lead to more (not less) meaning.

On a much more mundane level, a number of businesses are testing out this theoretical proposition in very practical ways. Tom Chappell, for example, of Tom's of Maine has been most explicit. In describing what he calls managing by the "Middle Way," he writes:

The Middle Way is not balance, nor is it a kind of compromise. It's a course that keeps in view competing aims: working efficiently versus taking time out for respect; making money versus being kind; having a kick-ass attitude versus having patience. The Middle Way is not "this way" or "that way," either-or; it's *one way that integrates both.* How is it that Buddha is serene yet mighty? How is it that Christ is meek yet majestic? It's because of how they did things—it's because of the practice of the Middle Way in their lives. . . . Like a boatman navigating a swirling river, Tom's of Maine has to steer between analysis and intuition, between our goals of profit and social responsibility, between softball and hardball. (1993, pp. 184–185)

It might just be the case that we can have our cake and eat it, too. For many companies, higher levels of social responsibility lead to more profits (Pava and Krausz, 1995). Consumer products can be designed not just to sell but to make consumers' lives better. For many employees, work is already a kind of play. To the extent that real, live social experiments like Tom's of Maine (and other values-led companies) succeed, this second interpretive stance is strengthened.

THE LAST WORD (FOR NOW)

To conclude, in a "consummatory experience" (from the word consummate—to bring to completion or perfection), according to Philip Selznick (following John Dewey), means partake of ends, and the distinction between them is purposely blurred. "The most complete union of means and ends occurs when, as in love, friendship, play, and art, process and outcome are indistinguishable" (Selznick, 1992, p. 328). Ultimately, an ethical organization is a place where consummatory experiences are rampant. Certainly, business organizations are good because they give each one of us, as individuals, good things. But, perhaps more importantly, business organizations, in themselves, are one of our culture's greatest goods, or at least someday they might be.

Works Cited

Abrahams, Jeffrey. 1995. *The Mission Statement Book*. Berkeley, CA: Ten Speed Press.

Ainslie, George. 1985. "Beyond Microeconomics: Conflict among Interests in a Multiple Self as a Determinant of Value." In Jon Elster, ed., *The Multiple Self*. Cambridge: Cambridge University Press, pp. 133–175.

Akerlof, George. 1979. "The Case against Conservative Macroeconomics: An Inaugural Lecture." *Economica*, Vol. 46, pp. 219–237.

Akerlof, George. 1983. "Loyalty Filters." *American Economic Review*, Vol. 73, No. 1, pp. 54–63.

Audi, Robert. Summer 1989. "The Separation of Church and State and the Obligations of Citizenship." *Philosophy and Public Affairs*, Vol. 18, pp. 259–296.

Audi, Robert. Winter 1991. "Religious Commitment and Secular Reason: A Reply to Professor Weithman." *Philosophy and Public Affairs*, Vol. 20, pp. 66–76.

Badaracco, Joseph L., Jr. 1997. *Defining Moments: When Managers Must Choose Between Right and Right*. Boston: Harvard Business School Press.

Badaracco, Joseph L., Jr., and Richard R. Ellsworth. 1989. *Leadership and the Quest of Integrity*. Boston: Harvard Business School Press.

Becker, Gary S. 1976. *The Economic Approach to Human Behavior*. Chicago: University of Chicago Press.

Bennis, Warren, and Patricia Ward Biederman. 1997. *Organizing Genius: The Secrets of Creative Collaboration*. Reading, MA: Addison-Wesley.

Berlin, Isaiah. 1980. "The Originality of Machiavelli." In Henry Hardy, ed., *Against the Current*. New York: Viking Press.

Berger, Peter L., and Thomas Luckmann. 1967. *The Social Construction of Reality: A Treatise in the Sociology of Knowledge*. New York: Anchor Press.

Bloom, Alan. 1987. *The Closing of the American Mind*. New York: Simon and Schuster.

Boisjoly, Roger M. 1993. "Personal Integrity and Accountability." *Accounting Horizons*, Vol. 7, No. 1, pp. 59–69.

Bowie, Norman E. 1991. "Challenging the Egoistic Paradigm." *Business Ethics Quarterly*, Vol. 1, No. 1, pp. 1–21.

Carr, Albert Z. 1968. "Is Business Bluffing Ethical?" *Harvard Business Review*, Vol. 46. Reprinted in Peter Madsen and Jay M. Shafritz, eds., *Essentials of Business Ethics*. New York: Penguin Books, 1990, pp. 62–78.

Chappell, Tom. 1993. *The Soul of a Business: Managing for Profit and the Common Good*. New York: Bantam Books.

Chernow, Ron. 1998. *Titan: The Life of John D. Rockefeller, Sr*. New York: Random House.

Cohen, Ben, and Jerry Greenfield. 1997. *Ben & Jerry's Double-Dip*. New York: Simon and Schuster.

Collins, James C., and Jerry I. Porras. 1997. *Built to Last: Successful Habits of Visionary Companies*. New York: HarperBusiness.

Cunningham, Lawrence A., ed. 1997. *The Essays of Warren Buffett: Lessons for Corporate America*. New York: Cardozo Law Review.

De George, Richard T. 1986. "Theological Ethics and Business Ethics." *Journal of Business Ethics*, Vol. 5, pp. 421–432.

Donaldson, Thomas, and Lee Preston. 1995. "The Stakeholder Theory of the Corporation: Concepts, Evidence, and Implications." *Academy of Management Review*, Vol. 20, No. 1, pp. 65–91.

Dowie, Mark. September–October 1977. "Pinto Madness." *Mother Jones*, pp. 18, 20.

Drucker, P. F. 1989. *The New Realities: In Government and Politics/In Economics and Business/In Society and World View*. New York: Harper and Row.

Drucker, Peter. 1993. *Post-Capitalist Society*. New York: HarperBusiness.

Dumaine, Brian. December 26, 1994. "Why Do We Work?" *Fortune*.

Dworkin, Ronald. 1985. *A Matter of Principle*. Cambridge: Harvard University Press.

Edelman, Murray. 1964. *The Symbolic Use of Politics*. Urbana: University of Illinois Press.

Edvinsson, Leif, and Michael S. Malone. 1997. *Intellectual Capital: Realizing Your Company's True Value by Finding Its Hidden Brainpower*. New York: HarperBusiness.

Elliott, Robert. 1992. "The Third Wave Breaks on the Shores of Accounting." *Accounting Horizons*, Vol. 6, No. 2, pp. 61–85.

Entine, Jon. September/October 1994. "Shattered Image: Is the Body Shop Too Good to Be True?" *Business Ethics.*

Epstein, Marc J. 1996. *Measuring Corporate Environmental Performance.* Chicago: Irwin.

Etzioni, Amitai. 1988. *The Moral Dimension: Toward a New Economics.* New York: Free Press.

Etzioni, Amitai. 1996a. *The New Golden Rule: Community and Morality in a Democratic Society.* New York: Basic Books.

Etzioni, Amitai. 1996b. "The Responsive Community: A Communitarian Perspective." *American Sociological Review*, Vol. 61, No. 1, pp. 1–11.

Ewing, David. 1977. "An Employee Bill of Rights." Reprinted in W. Michael Hoffman and Robert E. Frederick, *Business Ethics.* New York: McGraw-Hill, pp. 257–263.

Evan, William M., and R. Edward Freeman. 1988. "A Stakeholder Theory of the Modern Corporation: Kantian Capitalism." Reprinted in W. Michael Hoffman and Robert E. Frederick, *Business Ethics.* New York: McGraw-Hill, pp. 145–154.

Frank, Robert H. 1988. *Passions within Reason: The Strategic Role of the Emotions.* New York and London: W. W. Norton.

Frederick, William C., James E. Post, and Keith Davis. 1992. *Business and Society: Corporate Strategy, Public Policy, Ethics.* 7th ed. New York: McGraw Hill.

Friedman, Milton. 1962. *Capitalism and Freedom.* Chicago: University of Chicago Press.

Friedman, Milton. September 13, 1970. "A Friedman Doctrine—The Social Responsibility of Business Is to Increase Its Profits." *New York Times Magazine*, pp. 32–33, 123–125.

Friedman, Milton, and Rose Friedman. 1980. *Free to Choose.* New York: Avon Books.

Fromm, Erich. 1955. *The Sane Society.* London: Routledge and Kegan Paul.

Goldberg, Jeffrey. June 21, 1998. "Big Tobacco's Endgame." *New York Times Magazine*, pp. 36–42, 58–62.

Goodpaster, Kenneth E. 1991. "Business Ethics and Stakeholder Analysis." *Business Ethics Quarterly*, Vol. 1, No. 1, pp. 53–74.

Goodpaster, Kenneth E. 1994. "In Defense of a Paradox." *Business Ethics Quarterly*, Vol. 4, No. 4, pp. 423–429.

Greenawalt, Kent. 1988. *Religious Convictions and Political Choice.* New York and Oxford: Oxford University Press.

Greenawalt, Kent. 1990. "Religious Convictions and Political Choice: Some Further Thoughts." *Depaul Law Review*, Vol. 39, pp. 1019–1046.

Gutmann, Amy. 1993. "The Challenge of Multiculturalism in Political Ethics." *Philosophy and Public Affairs*, Vol. 22, No. 3, pp. 171–205.

Hartman, David. 1978. *Joy and Responsibility: Israel, Modernity, and the Renewal of Israel.* Jerusalem: Ben-Zwi-Ponser and Shalom Hartman Institute.

Hartman, Edwin. 1996. *Organizational Ethics and the Good Life*. New York: Oxford University Press.

Havel, Vaclav. 1992. *Summer Meditations*. New York: Alfred A Knopf.

Hemingway, Ernest. 1952. *The Old Man and the Sea*. New York: Charles Scribner's Sons.

Herberg, Will. 1951 *Judaism and Modern Man*. New York: Farrar, Straus, and Cudahy.

Heschel, Abraham Joshua. 1951. *The Sabbath: Its Meaning for Modern Man*. New York: Farrar, Straus, and Giroux.

Heschel, Abraham Joshua. 1955. *God in Search of Man: A Philosophy of Judaism*. New York: Harper and Row.

Heschel, Abraham Joshua. 1965. *Who Is Man?* Stanford, CA: Stanford University Press.

Hoffman, W. Michael. 1995. "The Ford Pinto." In W. Michael Hoffman and Robert E. Frederick, *Business Ethics*. New York: McGraw-Hill, pp. 552–558.

Hoffman, W. Michael. 1998. "Ethics Officers Association, 1995." Reprinted in Laura Pincus Hartman, ed., *Perspectives in Business Ethics*. Chicago: Irwin/McGraw-Hill, pp. 399–401.

Jensen, Michael C., and William H. Meckling. October 1976. "The Theory of the Firm: Managerial Behavior, Agency Costs, and Ownership Structure." *Journal of Financial Economics*, Vol. 3, pp. 305–360.

Jensen, Michael C., and William H. Meckling. 1994. "The Nature of Man." *Journal of Applied Corporate Finance*, Vol. 7, No. 2, pp. 4–19.

Kahneman, Daniel, Jack L. Knetsch, and Richard Thaler. 1986. "Fairness as a Constraint on Profit Seeking: Entitlements in the Market." *American Economic Review*, Vol. 76, pp. 728–741.

Kaplan, Robert, and David P. Norton. 1996. *The Balanced Scorecard: Translating Strategy into Action*. Boston: Harvard Business School Press.

King, Martin Luther. April 1963. "Letter from Birmingham City Jail." Reprinted in James Melvin Washington, ed., *A Testament of Hope: The Essential Writings of Martin Luther King, Jr*. San Francisco: Harper and Row.

Ladd, John. 1970. "Morality and the Ideal of Rationality in Formal Organizations." *The Monist*, Vol. 54, pp. 489–499.

Lev, Baruch. 1994. "Baruch Lev Responds." *California Management Review*, Vol. 36, No. 2, pp. 140–141.

Levine, Aaron, and Moses L. Pava. 1999. *Jewish Business Ethics: The Firm and Its Stakeholders*. Northvale, NJ: Jason Aronson.

March, James. Autumn 1978. "Bounded Rationality, Ambiguity, and the Engineering Choice." *Bell Journal of Economics*, Vol. 9, No. 2, pp. 587–608.

March, James, with the assistance of Chip Heath. 1994. *A Primer on Decision Making: How Decisions Happen*. New York: Free Press.

Maslow, Abraham. 1943. "A Theory of Human Motivation." Reprinted in Jay Shafritz and J. Steven Ott, eds., *Classics of Organization Theory*. Pacific Grove, CA: Brooks/Cole, 1992.

Maslow, Abraham. 1954. *Motivation and Personality*. New York: Harper.

Maslow, Abraham. 1968. *Toward a Psychology of Being*. Princeton: Van Nostrand.

McCoy, Bowen. September/October 1983. "The Parable of the Sadhu." *Harvard Business Review*, Vol. 61. Reprinted in Peter Madsen and Jay M. Shafritz, eds., *Essentials of Business Ethics*. New York: Penguin Books, 1990, pp. 190–200.

Michels, Robert. 1962. *Political Parties: A Sociological Study of the Oligarchical Tendencies of Modern Democracy*. Glencoe, NY: Free Press.

Milgram, Stanley. 1974. *Obedience to Authority*. New York: Harper Colophon Books.

Nash, Laura. 1990. *Good Intentions Aside: A Manager's Guide to Resolving Ethical Problems*. Cambridge: Harvard Business School Press.

Novak, Michael. 1982. *The Spirit of Democratic Capitalism*. New York: Simon and Schuster.

Nozick, Robert. 1993. *The Nature of Rationality*. Princeton, NJ: Princeton University Press.

Okun, Arthur. 1981. *Prices and Quantities: A Macroeconomic Analysis*. Washington, DC: Brookings Institution.

Pava, Moses L. 1997a. *Business Ethics: A Jewish Perspective*. Hoboken, NJ: Ktav and Yeshiva University Press.

Pava, Moses L. May 1997b. "Corporate Social Responsibilities: Yesterday and Today." Paper presented at Symposium in Honor of Clarence Walton, American College, Philadelphia.

Pava, Moses L. 1997c. "Religious Business Ethics as Interpretation: A Jewish Perspective." *International Journal of Value-Based Management*, Vol. 10, pp. 9–29.

Pava, Moses L., and Joshua Krausz. 1994. "Corporate Responsibilities: Beyond 'Information Disclosure Strategy.'" *California Management Review*, Vol. 36, No. 2, pp. 134–139.

Pava, Moses L., and Joshua Krausz. 1995. *Corporate Responsibility and Financial Performance: The Paradox of Social Cost*. Westport, CT: Quorum Books.

Pava, Moses L., and Joshua Krausz. 1996. "The Association between Corporate Social Responsibility and Financial Performance: The Paradox of Social Cost." *The Journal of Business Ethics*, Vol. 15, pp. 321–357.

Pava, Moses L. and Joshua Krausz. 1997. "Criteria for Evaluating the Legitimacy of Corporate Social Responsibility." *Journal of Business Ethics*, Vol. 16, pp. 337–347.

Pava, Moses L., and Joshua Krausz. 1998. "Annual Reports as a Medium for Voluntarily Signaling and Justifying Corporate Social Responsibility Activities." *Research on Accounting Ethics*, Vol. 4, pp. 1–27.

Peters, Thomas J. 1978. "Symbols, Patterns, and Settings: An Optimistic Case for Getting Things Done." *Organizational Dynamics*, Vol. 7, pp. 3–23.

Pfeffer, Jeffrey. 1981. "Management as Symbolic Action: The Creation and Maintenance of Organizational Paradigms." *Research in Organizational Behavior*, Vol. 3, pp. 1–52.

Pollard, C. William. 1996. *The Soul of the Firm*. New York: HarperBusiness.

Post, James E., Edwin A. Murray, Robert B. Dickie, John F. Mahon, and Michael E. Jones. 1981. *Public Affairs Offices and Their Functions: Summary of Survey Responses*. Boston: Public Affairs Research Group, Boston University.

Preston, L. E. 1981. "Research on Corporate Social Reporting: Directions for Development." *Accounting, Organizations, and Society*, Vol. 6, No. 3, pp. 255–262.

Rawls, John. 1971. *A Theory of Justice*. Cambridge: Harvard University Press.

Rawls, John. 1993. *Political Liberalism*. New York: Columbia University Press.

Reid, Thomas R. 1965. "Public Affairs: A Company Program." In *Broadening the Dimensions of Public Affairs*. New York: Conference Board.

Schein, Edgar H. 1985. *Organizational Culture and Leadership*. San Francisco: Jossey-Bass. Reprinted in Jay Shafritz and J. Steven Ott, eds., *Classics of Organization Theory*. Pacific Grove, CA: Brooks/Cole.

Selznick, Philip. 1957, 1984. *Leadership in Administration*. Berkeley: University of California Press.

Selznick, Philip. 1992. *The Moral Commonwealth: Social Theory and the Promise of Community*. Berkeley: University of California Press.

Smith, C. May–June 1994. "The New Corporate Philanthropy." *Harvard Business Review*, pp. 105–116.

Soloveitchik, Joseph B. 1965. *The Lonely Man of Faith*. New York: Doubleday.

Soloveitchik, Joseph B. 1967. "Confrontation." In Norman Lamm and Walter S. Wurzburger, eds., *A Treasury of "Tradition."* New York: Hebrew, pp. 55–80.

Soloveitchik, Joseph B. 1983. *Halakhic Man*. Philadelphia: Jewish Publication Society of America.

Solow, Robert. 1980. "On Theories of Unemployment." *American Economic Review*, Vol. 70, pp. 1–11.

Solum, Lawrence B. 1990. "Faith and Justice." *Depaul Law Review*, Vol. 39, pp. 1083–1106.

Stark, Andrew. May–June 1993. "What's the Matter with Business Ethics?" *Harvard Business Review*, pp. 38–48.

Stigler, George J., and Gary S. Becker. 1977. "De Gustibus Non Est Disputandum." *The American Economic Review*, Vol. 67, pp. 76–90.

Stone, Christopher. 1975. "Where the Law Ends: The Social Control of Corporate Behavior." Reprinted in W. Michael Hoffman and Robert E. Frederick, *Business Ethics*. New York: McGraw-Hill, pp. 141–145.

Surowiecki, James. June 15, 1998. "The Billion Dollar Blade." *The New Yorker*, pp. 43–49.

Taylor, Charles. 1995. *Philosophical Arguments*. Cambridge: Harvard University Press.

Tillich, Paul. 1957. *The Dynamics of Faith*. New York: Harper and Row.

Toffler, Barbara Ley. 1986. *Tough Choices: Managers Talk Ethics*. New York: John Wiley and Sons.

Walton, Clarence. 1967. *Corporate Social Responsibilities*. Belmont, CA: Wadsworth.

Walzer, Michael. 1987. *Interpretation and Social Criticism*. Cambridge: Harvard University Press.

Weber, Leonard J. 1996. "Citizenship and Democracy: The Ethics of Corporate Lobbying." *Business Ethics Quarterly*, Vol. 6, No. 2, pp. 253–259.

Weber, Max. 1954. *Max Weber on Law in Economy and Society*. Cambridge: Harvard University Press.

Weithman, Paul J. Winter 1991. "The Separation of Church and State: Some Questions for Professor Audi." *Philosophy and Public Affairs*, Vol. 20, pp. 52–65.

Wood, Donna. 1994. *Business and Society*. New York: HarperCollins College.

Index

About the Author

MOSES L. PAVA holds the Alvin Einbender Chair in Business Ethics at the Sy Syms School of Business, Yeshiva University, New York. Dr. Pava is recognized internationally as one of the leading academic authorities on business ethics and has lectured in Japan, Israel, and across the United States. Published widely in a variety of academic and professional journals, he is coauthor of *Corporate Responsibility and Financial Performance* (1995, with Joshua Krausz), which was cited by *Choice* as one of the outstanding books in business, management, and labor for 1996.